D0070658

Bestest

The Life of Peyton Tooke Anderson, Jr.

Bestest

The Life of Peyton Tooke Anderson, Jr.

By

Jaclyn Weldon White

MERCER UNIVERSITY PRESS
MACON, GEORGIA
25TH ANNIVERSARY

ISBN 0-86554-935-4
MUP/H676

© 2005 Mercer University Press
1400 Coleman Avenue
Macon, Georgia 31207
All rights reserved

First Edition.

∞The paper used in this publication meets the minimum requirements
of American National Standard for Information
Sciences—Permanence of Paper for Printed Library Materials,
ANSI Z39.48-1992.

Library of Congress Cataloging-in-Publication Data

White, Jaclyn Weldon.
The life of Peyton Tooke Anderson, Jr. / by Jaclyn Weldon
White.-- 1st ed.
p. cm.
Includes bibliographical references and index.
ISBN 0-86554-935-4 (hardback : alk. paper)
1. Anderson, Peyton Tooke, 1907-1988. 2. Newspaper
editors—United States—Biography. 3. Publishers and
publishing—United States—Biography.
I. Title.
PN4874.A533W45 2005
070.4'1'092—dc22

2005002193

Contents

In memory of D. C. and Nannie Mae White, two special people who welcomed me into their family with love and laughter.

Prologue

The headline in the 23 September 1990 *Macon Telegraph* announced "Anderson Foundation Puts Up Cash for City." The accompanying story contained a brief biography of Peyton T. Anderson, Jr., and a list of some of the recently formed Foundation's beneficiaries. But it was the photo of Anderson—a man of advanced years grinning at the camera as if he knew some wonderful secret about life itself—that captured the reader's attention. Who had this man been and why was he so happy?

The impact Peyton Anderson had on Macon, Georgia, is difficult to quantify. He was a successful businessman, a loving family man, a civic leader, a trusted friend and a philanthropist. What drives a man to amass a huge fortune during his lifetime? What leads him to care so much for his community that, at his death, most of that fortune is used to establish a foundation for the benefit of his hometown? To understand the man and why he acted as he did, one must understand the history of the Anderson family and the remarkable life led by Peyton Anderson, Jr.

ACKNOWLEDGMENTS

This book could not have been written without the kind assistance of the Peyton Anderson family, including Katherine Anderson, Deyerle McNair, Laura Nelle O'Callaghan, Reid Hanson and Denny O'Callaghan Jones. Friends and associates of Mr. Anderson who contributed to this book, freely sharing their memories, include Juanita Jordan, Alvah Chapman, Jim Chapman, John Comer, Margena Dunlap, Taffy Folsom, Jack and Sarah Eich, Barbara and Carlton Hunnicutt, Bill Matthews, Denny McCrary, Reg Murphy, Berma Ramfjiord, David Redding, Jr., Ed Sell, Jr., Ed Sell III, Del Ward, Harold Wood, Jim Wooten, Ann Youmans, and Mason and Miriam Zuber.

Muriel Jackson of the Middle Georgia Regional Library provided invaluable help and advice in retrieving information from the library file,s and the *Macon Telegraph* and *Macon News* archives. And finally the Bibb County Clerk of Court's Office staff was most generous in their help locating information in the county's probate files.

A Peyton Tooke Anderson Jr. Photograph Album

Vineville School, second grade, 1914. Peyton Anderson, Jr. 4th from left, back row.

Peyton Anderson, Jr., Nell Anderson, PT Anderson, Laura Nelle Anderson on the front porch of their English Avenue home, ca. 1916.

Peyton Anderson, Jr., United
States Naval Academy, 1925.

Katherine (Katty) and Deyerle
Anderson, East Bay Street,
Charleston, South Carolina, 1942.

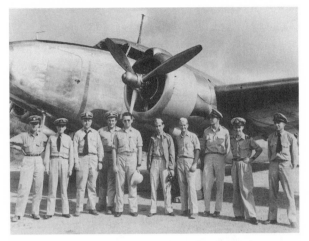

Peyton Anderson, Jr., third from left, South Pacific, 1944.

Peyton, Deyerle, Kat and Katty Anderson in the kitchen of
their Oakcliff Road house, late 1940's.

The *Macon Telegraph* Building,
Cherry Street, ca. 1948.

Fleet Admiral Chester Nimitz
awards Peyton Anderson, Jr. the
Bronze Star, April, 1946.

Peyton Anderson, Jr. and Carmage Walls, change of ownership of The Macon Telegraph, January 3, 1951.

Carl Vinson's first flight, Warner Robins Air Force Base, 1951. L-R General Elwood Quesada, Peyton Anderson, Jr., General Ignaco, US Representative Carl Vinson, Secretary of the Air Force Stuart Symington, Air Force Chief of Staff General Hoyt Vandenberg, US Representative Lyndon B. Johnson.

Peyton Anderson, Jr., outgoing president, and Harry B. Bradley, president elect, Southern Newspaper Publishers Association, mid 1950's.

The new *Macon Telegraph* and News Building, 1961.

Presentation of plaque from his employees to Peyton Anderson, Jr., April 7, 1961.

Peyton and Kat Anderson on vacation, 1961.

US Representative Carl Vinson, Governor Carl Sanders, President Lyndon B. Johnson, Peyton Anderson, Jr., October 26, 1964.

Peyton Anderson, Jr. with President Lyndon Johnson during campaign appearance in Macon, October 26, 1964.

Coat of Arms for Peyton's Place,
Lake Sinclair.

Newspapers being delivered by helicopter, 1968.

Kat and Peyton Anderson, Jr.,
late 1960's.

Peyton Anderson, Jr., press room,
Macon Telegraph and news, mid
1960's.

Peyton Anderson, Jr.'s honorary
membership card, Bibb County
Sheriff's Office, 1968.

The first yacht, Peyton's Place II,
1970.

Portrait of Peyton Anderson, Jr., unveiled, April 27, 1974.

The second yacht, Peyton's Place II, 1974.

Peyton Anderson, Jr., with Hoi Toi statue, gift from David and Blanche Redding, Christmas, 1974.

Fishing trip, Chub Cay, June 1980. L-R Jason Bleibtreu, Adam Bleibtreu, Reid Hanson, Peyton Hanson, Peyton Anderson, Jr., Joshua Bleibtreu.

Christmas, 1981.

Evelyn and Peyton Anderson, Jr., 1984.

Board of Trustees, Peyton Anderson Foundation, ca. 1993.

1

The Andersons Come to Macon

Christopher and Laura Tooke Anderson had eight children—five daughters and three sons. They raised their large family in Hawkinsville, Georgia, during the last quarter of the nineteenth century. The aftermath of the Civil War had brought hard times to all the southern states and jobs were not easy to find. The Andersons' eldest son, Eugene left home in 1884 when he was only seventeen years old for the nearby town of Macon. There he found work with the *Macon Telegraph* newspaper as a printer's apprentice.

Over the next four years, his brothers William and Peyton joined him there, also finding jobs with the *Telegraph*. Peyton, the youngest, earned four dollars a week as one of the composing room crew.

Macon was an exciting place for three young men who'd been raised in the countryside. New streetcars traversed the downtown area and, in 1897, the Spring Street Bridge was completed, linking the two sides of the Ocmulgee River. Business was flourishing.

The Anderson men did well in this environment. They were bright and ambitious and unafraid of hard work. By 1895 Eugene had risen to the rank of city editor.

William, now know as W. T., was promoted to composing room foreman, but the title was misleading. A young man who was willing to step in wherever he was needed, he soon became a little of everything. When the weather forecast failed to arrive in time from the Weather Bureau one night, he went outside, looked at the stars and simply made one up. Another time a veteran editorial writer showed up for work so drunk that he couldn't do his job. W. T. hurriedly went back through some old newspapers, found bits and pieces of previous, uncontroversial columns and wrote the editorial himself.

Peyton, whose nickname was now P. T., was far from certain that he wanted a career in the newspaper business. So in 1894, he took a job with the railroad. Soon afterwards, he and W.T. purchased a house at 139 Rose Park and moved their sisters there from Hawkinsville.

In 1895, Eugene married Nina Warren and they moved into a house on Appleton Avenue, just off College Street. W. T. was only two years behind his older brother in becoming a married man. He wed Elizabeth Anderson and they took up residence at 220 Vineville Avenue. It was not until 1906 that P. T. married. His bride was Nell Griswold, a recent Wesleyan College graduate. The newlyweds set up housekeeping in a small upstairs apartment on Rose Park near P. T.'s sisters.

Streetcars were a recent addition to Macon and, during the hot summer of 1906, labor problems erupted. The operators went on strike and were soon joined by carpenters and roundhouse employees from the railroads. The disagreement grew more and more heated. When, in mid-August, the tracks were greased, derailing a car and shutting down the entire line, the dispute went into arbitration; but before an agreement could be reached, the violence escalated. In September there was a bloodless shoot-out on the streets of Macon between strike sympathizers and company employees. After that, both sides were eager to reach an accord and, within weeks, a contract had been signed and the cars were running once more.

P. T. rose to the rank of Chief Clerk for the Central of Georgia Railroad and seemed positioned for a bright career there. He and Nell had their first child on 9 April 1907 and named him Peyton Tooke Anderson, Jr. Their second child, Laura Nelle, was born in

1910 and the young couple began looking for a larger home. They purchased a house at 165 English Avenue.

In addition to his nighttime duties at the *Telegraph*, Eugene Anderson had been attending day classes at Mercer University. He eventually came to the conclusion that his destiny was education. He took a job as a teacher at Mercer and, in 1907, purchased the Georgia Alabama Business School from Professor E. C. Martin, who had founded it in 1889.

The latter years of the decade were financially uncertain. In December 1907, there was a stock market panic. Only J. P. Morgan's pumping millions into the market saved it from collapse. But W. T. Anderson wasn't unduly concerned about what was happening in New York. His focus was much more local. He'd been quietly buying *Macon Telegraph* stock for several years and planned to own the paper eventually. When in 1909 he was named general manager, he persuaded his younger brother to come back to work at the *Telegraph* as circulation manager. Although it represented a small cut in pay, P. T. returned to the paper, with the guarantee that he'd receive a commission on any increase in sales. He believed he could make a positive difference in that area. He was right. In one year, the circulation doubled to nearly 14,000—over a third of the entire population of the city.

It wasn't only the newspaper that was growing. In 1910, Macon experienced its greatest expansion since its founding in 1823. Building boomed. The Dempsey Hotel was erected and construction started on the Post Office Building. In September, over 2,000 people gathered downtown to witness the lighting of Macon's "white way." Local dignitaries crowded onto a platform built in front of the Joseph N. Neel Company. When the switch was thrown, light flooded Cherry Street and the crowd cheered.

The following year, the *Macon Telegraph* moved to its new home at 452 Cherry Street. It was a spacious steel and concrete building with the latest equipment, including a large four-deck Goss press.

Ten thousand people attended the opening celebration and watched the newspaper being printed right before them.

From across the world came the rumblings of war. On 2 August 1914 Germany invaded Luxembourg. Two days later, Britain and Belgium declared war on Germany. In the United States, people kept an uneasy eye on the European situation, but it seemed very far removed from their everyday life. In Macon, the owner of the *Telegraph* had died and W. T. was ready to make his move to acquire it.

By November of that year, he and P. T. had saved and borrowed $54,000 with which to purchase the remaining stock. In partnership with his brother, W. T. bought and completely reorganized the paper. He assumed the position of owner, editor and publisher. P. T. was made vice president and business manager and George Long was named managing editor and editorial writer.

W. T. was almost as interested in civic affairs as he was in business. He was elected to the school board, served on the committee to arrange for the purchase of the city waterworks, served as vice president of the Macon Rotary Club, and was a member of the Dixie Highway Commission. His concern extended to all of Macon's citizens.

At a time when most white men dealt with blacks only as servants or employees, W. T. was an exception. He became interested in the Fort Valley School, an agricultural college for black students in a nearby town. Each year the school held its Ham and Egg Show, which grew to be one of the best agricultural expositions in the South. W. T. publicized the work being done at the school and advertised the event in his newspaper. He even went to other city leaders and persuaded them to help him find prizes for the show and financial aid for the students.

W. T. and P. T. were early members of the fledgling Southern Newspaper Publishers Association. In 1915, W. T. was elected president of that organization. The SNPA press release described him as "always a strong-minded dissenter from the fad of the moment."

P. T. Anderson was often called upon to head up fundraising drives for local civic and charitable organizations. The year he was director of the Macon Community Chest was the first one in which that organization achieved its monetary goal.

Eugene Anderson had also become an influential man in the city. He served on the board of trustees formed to control the planning and building of the Washington Memorial Library and led the 1916 drive for membership in the Macon chapter of the Red Cross. In 1916, his wife Nina died and the following year he married Mrs. Annie Speer Burr.

People in Macon watched along with the rest of the world as conditions in Europe deteriorated. Then in 1917 the United States entered the war. When American boys began training at nearby Camp Wheeler, the *Telegraph* started publishing a Sunday magazine specifically for soldiers called *Trench and Camp*. It carried military news and personal articles. When the armistice was signed in November 1918, the *Telegraph* rejoiced with the rest of the country. P. T. Anderson was on a committee formed in 1919 to celebrate the return of soldiers to Macon, particularly the 151st Machine Gun Battalion.

As the decade drew to a close, the publishing industry experienced a growing shortage of trained printers. Union rules provided that a newspaper could have only one trainee, or apprentice, for every four to five journeymen printers. The publishers suspected the reason for this rule was to keep the number of qualified printers so low that the unions would almost be able to dictate the terms of their contracts. In response to the situation, W. T. Anderson proposed to the Southern Newspaper Publishers Association that they help him start a printers' school. They agreed, and in 1919 the SNPA entered into a contract with Eugene Anderson's Georgia Alabama School of Business to establish the Macon School of

Typesetting. W. T. headed the oversight committee and Eugene was the director. Tuition for the training was $150. The printers' school operated in Macon until the SNPA support ended in 1924. Then the operation was adopted by the American Newspaper Publishers Association and moved to Nashville, Tennessee, where it became the Southern School of Printing.

P. T. Anderson was a big, burly man with a ready smile and a pleasant speaking voice. He was an accomplished businessman and a dynamic civic leader. First and foremost, though, he was a devoted family man. Peyton, Jr., and Laura Nelle were happy in the English Avenue house. There were a lot of children up and down the block and they were in and out of each other's houses all the time. They skated and rode bicycles and attended the Vineville School. Each morning Peyton and Laura Nelle left the house and walked together down the street, through the woods and across the little stream to get to the school on Vineville Avenue.

Nell Anderson believed the secret to staying healthy was getting plenty of fresh air. She saw to it that this was accomplished by having her family use the sleeping porch all year round. It was furnished with two double beds. Laura Nelle shared one with her mother and Peyton slept with P. T. During the summer, this was the only place in the house where cool breezes made the heat bearable enough to sleep. But winter is a cold season, even in Macon. The porch had casement windows, but Nell would not hear of them being closed. When the temperature dropped, blankets were piled on the beds to keep the family warm overnight.

P. T. had an arrangement with several of the newspaper deliverymen. During cold weather, they'd come by the Anderson house before daybreak, let themselves in and get the fire going in the fireplace. Then they'd go deliver their papers. When the family rose an hour later, they'd hurry into the house to dress by the warmth of the established fire. Peyton and Laura Nelle never knew the names of the men who came to light the fires. Instead, the children referred to them by the numbers of their delivery routes.

When P. T. traveled, he often took Nell with him. Once or twice a year they went to New York City so that he could meet with executives from the John M. Branham Company, the advertising agency that represented the *Telegraph* nationally. Laura Nelle and Peyton didn't accompany them when they were small, staying instead with relatives in Macon. June 1912 was such a time. Two-year-old Laura Nelle stayed with P. T.'s widowed sister Lela Key and her sisters at the Rose Park house. Peyton stayed with another aunt and uncle, Alma and Oren Massey. Even at age five, he was a particular and determined little boy. When he arrived at their house, his aunt showed him to his room. As she wrote his parents in a letter, "He came with an air of profound importance." Informing her that he could unpack himself, he opened his suitcase. Whistling, he arranged his clothes neatly in dresser drawers, then pulled out a nightshirt and held it up for his cousins to see. "You want to see something cute?" he asked. His aunt had to bite her lips to keep from laughing out loud.

As they grew older, their parents occasionally took the children on the New York trips. The hotels provided them with rooms as payment for outstanding advertising bills. Laura Nelle and Peyton were intrigued by this arrangement and thought it was grand that their parents got so many things "for free." P. T. made sure they didn't keep that illusion for very long. "We paid a lot for those things one way or another," he'd tell them. "They sure aren't free. You don't get anything for free."

The *Macon Telegraph* was a morning paper and P. T. was often required to work late into the evenings. So the family's main meal was a large dinner served in the middle of the day when he could come home and join them. And some evenings Nell took her two children to town where they would meet P. T. about eight o'clock for supper. One of their favorite restaurants was Ed Loh's Cafe on Mulberry Street. To the Anderson children, it was the height of elegance. It was there that they first had Spanish omelets, served with hash-browned potatoes. Laura Nelle was sure it was the best food in the world.

It was the Spanish omelets that first involved the Anderson children in cooking. Peyton was especially interested in learning to prepare them. Nell encouraged them both, and by the time he was nine and Laura Nelle was six, they were occasionally allowed to prepare supper by themselves. Their specialty, of course, was Spanish omelets, but they also produced huge sandwiches with multiple ingredients.

During the summer vacation of 1916, Peyton had his first paying job. At age nine, he worked as an office boy at the *Macon Telegraph*. Even then, he loved the bustle of the newsroom, the huge presses, and the air of importance about the business itself. He saw the respect with which the employees regarded his uncle and his father. "Mr. W. T." and "Mr. P. T." seemed to be pretty important folks. Peyton wanted to be important, too.

2

From Macon to Annapolis

The 1920s was a decade of hope and soaring expectation. The war that had cost so much in human suffering and resources was over. The troops were home, business was booming and the future was bright. There were, however, a few dark spots in the country.

The Ku Klux Klan was experiencing a revival. Setting themselves up as arbiters of morality, they randomly judged their fellow citizens and punished those that fell short of their standards. "Klan justice" came to Macon in early 1922. Local men were taken from their homes by gangs of masked men and beaten for their perceived transgressions. The reasons for such treatment varied. One victim was accused of drunkenness, another of abandoning his family, and yet another for running a house of prostitution. A banner day for the Klan was 9 August 1923; the vigilante gang attacked four different men in one night.

Macon wasn't the only town suffering from such activity. The state, in fact much of the nation, was being similarly victimized. Georgia Governor Clifford Walker posted a $500 reward for the capture of those involved and the Macon City Council matched that amount. Bibb County Sheriff James Hicks set up a special squad to apprehend the nightriders.

W. T. Anderson was greatly disturbed by these attacks and the seeming ability of the Klan to avoid justice. The *Telegraph* published front-page editorials condemning the floggings and suggesting that one or more of the incidents might have been prompted more by business rivalry than moral outrage. The Klan didn't easily tolerate such criticism. W. T. received death threats and even had a cross burned in front of his house, but the publisher of the *Macon Telegraph* was not intimidated. He printed a warning in his paper that he carried a pistol in his car and would welcome a confrontation. None came, and finally a number of arrests put a stop to the nighttime attacks.

For P. T. and Nell Anderson, life was good. The family business was doing well and they'd acquired part ownership of a farm and a quarry. P. T. made sure his family knew where their livelihood lay. There were strict rules for where they shopped. If a business didn't advertise with the *Telegraph*, the Andersons didn't shop there. They bought what they needed locally. "The money was earned in Macon," he would tell his children. "It should be spent in Macon."

When development began on 500 acres across the Ocmulgee River, P. T. was one of the first to purchase a lot and commission the building of a house on what was then a dirt road called Sunset Drive. The name would later be changed to Oakcliff Drive in the subdivision known as Shirley Hills. Soon after the purchase, construction began on what was to be an impressive house—two stories with a sweeping two-tiered staircase and imposing white columns across the front. Their English Avenue home sold quicker than expected—so quickly, in fact, that the new house was still far from ready.

"Well, we've got to move," P. T. told his family, "and the house isn't finished. Maybe we'll move to the Dempsey until it is."

The idea thrilled young Laura Nelle. She could think of nothing more glamorous than living at the fancy downtown hotel. But it wasn't to be. P. T. and Nell came up with another solution. In September 1922, the family moved from English Avenue into a small building on their Shirley Hills property that would eventually become the servants' quarters. They called it 'the little house.'

It was close living for a while. The house had only one room, a bath, and a small front porch. A double garage was attached to one side of the structure. They crowded beds and chairs into the single room and moved a stove and refrigerator into the garage. Conditions were so crowded that Peyton, who was then fifteen years old, elected to sleep outdoors. He set up a tent a short distance from the house. This arrangement worked well for a while. Then late one night he was awakened by the raucous scream of an owl. It frightened him so much he ran into the little house and refused to return to his tent. From then on he slept in the small structure with the rest of his family.

Nell Anderson wasn't at all bothered by the inconvenience of living in one small room with her family. With the help of a cook and yardman who came to the house daily, she kept their lives running on schedule and kept herself busy. An excellent seamstress, she even reupholstered an entire set of furniture while they were there, doing all of the work on the tiny porch.

Laura Nelle and Peyton had grown up calling each other Sister and Bubba, but they now came to the conclusion that such behavior was childish. They agreed to change the names they called each other. Sister would be called Nelle and Bubba would forever after be Pate.

If it had been up to Peyton, the Andersons would have never left their old neighborhood. He'd fallen for a girl who lived on Cleveland Avenue, only two streets away from their old house. Katherine McClure, known as Kat, was the daughter of Andrew and Julia McClure, and Peyton thought she was the most wonderful girl he would ever known. Now he was living a distant ten miles away from her, rather than ten minutes. And Peyton would soon be much farther away than that.

A few months after moving to Shirley Hills, he left Macon to attend Riverside Military Academy, a hundred miles north in Gainesville, Georgia. Peyton was one of a number of Macon students reporting that year. B. F. Merritt, Bob Kingman, and Monk

McAllister were among his classmates. He enjoyed Riverside and did well there, eventually being named captain of a company.

When Peyton came home for Christmas break, the move into the big house was complete. Happy as he was to be with his parents and sister again, he barely said hello to them before hurrying to the telephone. He picked up the receiver and told the operator, "963." His parents smiled indulgently as they recognized Kat McClure's number. Although separated, the two young people kept in close touch while Peyton was away. They wrote frequently and Kat traveled to Riverside several times to be his sponsor at homecomings and other events.

When he wasn't with Kat, much of Peyton's time at home was taken up by what his family called his gadgets. He loved machines of all kinds. He could repair almost any motor or electrical device and he particularly enjoyed rigging up contraptions to amaze his family. Laura Nelle was never completely comfortable in Peyton's room because of the wires that seemed to run everywhere. Pulling one turned on a light. Another set off a bell if the door were opened. She just tried not to touch anything when she was there.

Peyton graduated from Riverside Military Academy in 1924. He had planned to go to the University of Georgia, having already pledged to the fraternity Sigma Alpha Epsilon while attending high school in Macon. But his father had other ideas. He was determined that Peyton should attend one of the national military academies. Through Congressman Carl Vinson, he got an appointment to the Naval Academy. Before entering the Academy, Peyton spent one year at the Columbian Preparatory School in Washington, DC.

The Anderson brothers continued to be active in Macon's civic life. P. T. was one of the early leaders of the Masivic Club, a Masons-related organization that was founded in 1922, and in 1925 he became president of the Chamber of Commerce. W. T. was vice president of the local Federal Housing Authority, president of the Agricultural and Mechanical School of Barnesville and a trustee of the Herty Foundation. Eugene, always concerned with education, formed a local Illiteracy Commission and promoted the first adult reading classes ever held at the Willingham Cotton Mills.

The *Telegraph* grew larger every year. By 1925, the circulation was near 30,000. The paper employed ninety carriers who each delivered 150 papers a day. About that same time, the paper began running a "Colored News Page" and W. T. started what would be a lifelong campaign for economic opportunity for blacks.

Franklin D. Roosevelt was stricken with polio in 1921. Soon after that, he began traveling to Warm Springs, Georgia, for treatment of the disease. One of the people he got to know there was Thomas W. Loyless, a *Macon Telegraph* columnist. The two men became friends and in 1925 Loyless suggested that Roosevelt write some columns for the paper. The politician agreed and, for several months thereafter, his column "Roosevelt Says" appeared sporadically in the Macon paper. His subjects were diverse, ranging from immigration to civil service and national affairs.

The columns were well received by the paper's readers, and W. T. Anderson and Roosevelt began a friendship that would last for several years. When Roosevelt decided that Warm Springs should be developed, W. T. and other prominent local leaders joined him in the effort. The goal was to change Warm Springs from a destination for the sick to a vacation resort. Along with a large sanitarium and treatment facility at the springs, they envisioned a separate swimming pool and picnic area for the public, and hunting and fishing preserves.

In the fall of 1925, Peyton entered the Naval Academy. Although he hadn't initially wanted to attend the school, he adapted well to life there. His natural abilities and determination to excel, coupled with the military experience he'd received at Riverside, soon made him a leader in his class.

His roommate was a Savannah boy named Walter Parrish, known to one and all as Rags. The two quickly became friends and that friendship continued for the rest of their lives. Because of their association, Rags often visited Macon with Peyton. It was there that he met his future wife, Julia Lamar.

That winter, Laura Nelle was allowed to travel to New York with *Telegraph* circulation manager Roy Neal and his wife. It was an exciting trip for a fifteen-year-old girl. The highlight for her was the day they spent in Annapolis. Peyton looked so grown up in his uniform that his sister barely recognized him. He showed them around the campus and then visited with them in the reception room until late afternoon. He said goodbye to Laura Nelle and the Neals on the terrace of Bancroft Hall where his classmates had gathered before going to dinner. Then, right before his sister's eyes, Peyton turned into a military officer. He called the other boys to order. Under his command, they marched away to the dining hall. Laura Nelle had never before been so impressed with her brother.

The plebe year at the Naval Academy was a difficult one, full of hazing and hardship, but Peyton took it all in stride. When he went home for the Christmas holidays, P. T. was astonished. In four months it seemed that Peyton had grown from a boy to a young man.

P. T. wrote to his son after he returned to school in January. He began with some good-natured chiding, expressing sentiments familiar to any parent whose child has traveled away from home. "Your wire read 'Am writing tonight'. As your letter is not here, suppose the mails are delayed as a midshipman would not make a misstatement." Then his letter grew serious. "I don't believe since you have been born have I ever been any more pleased with you and your progress than right now. I hope you are as proud of me as your daddy as I am of you as my son." He went on to share future plans with him, confiding that he expected him to join the family business, but not before working in a larger market, such as New York or Chicago, to learn about foreign and national advertising. He signed the letter "love, Daddy."

As part of his Academy training, Peyton took part in several naval cruises to ports on the Atlantic coast, as well as Cuba and the Bahamas. During this time, Peyton developed a love for boating and being on the water that would never leave him.

While Peyton was in Annapolis, Kat McClure was a student at Hollins College in Virginia. The two continued to correspond regularly and spent as much time as they could together during holiday breaks. Over summer vacations, Peyton worked at the *Telegraph*, where his father saw to it that he received experience in all the departments and his uncle drilled into him the law for newspapermen as he saw it.

"Many of our readers take no other paper. Our paper in that case has an additional responsibility not to mislead our readers," W. T. told him many times. "This makes it all the more important that we keep all news stories free from bias, point only in truth, and present all legitimate news.

"Subscribers are limited stockholders. Their dividends are in the service we render them through printing news that may affect their interests so they may arrange protections.

"In securing and preparing news, pay no attention whatever to editorial positions or papers. It is up to the editorial staff to take chances with the news breaks as they actually develop. The news department is not supposed to nor expected to bolster or support any editorial declarations or arguments."

W. T. often told Peyton something that would become the basis of the younger man's philosophy of life. "Treat the lowliest and the highest with the same consideration you would ask for yourself or show to your own family if you were called upon to write a story about one of them. Let us always endeavor to make people and not to break them."

Late in the summer of 1927, Peyton returned to Annapolis and was preparing for his next year at the Academy when he injured his knee playing intramural sports. He wasn't concerned at first. He'd shaken off injuries before, but this one was different. Rather than improving with time, it worsened. After more than a week, he went home to Macon. Soon afterwards, P. T. took him to Dr. Michael Hoke in Atlanta. After a thorough examination, the doctor reported that Peyton had damaged the internal semi-lunar cartilage in his knee. Surgery to remove the cartilage was recommended. "At your age," Hoke told the boy, "removal of it usually results in a knee that is capable of standing stress and strain."

Peyton went back to Annapolis, unsure of what would happen next. For the Naval Academy to be satisfied, his recovery had to be total. In September, he was sent to the Naval Hospital for observation and treatment. There he was poked and prodded and counseled. The people in charge were certain that he should have the surgery, but they weren't prepared to perform it there. Instead they wanted him to go home, have the surgery and then return to the Academy if and when his recovery was complete.

While Peyton wanted to stay at the Academy, he feared that surgery could make his condition worse rather than better. The doctors reassured him that such a thing probably wouldn't happen, but they couldn't guarantee him a full recovery. Peyton couldn't make up his mind. He wrote letters to his family, first leaning one way, then the other.

P. T. was growing impatient. "I have not been able to figure from your messages and letters what you really want to do," he wrote to Peyton on September 29. "I thought you had decided you wanted to leave the Academy and come home to work and arranged things accordingly. Now I understand that you want to stay if you can make it stick. Either way is all right with me."

His father laid out the options of staying, coming home to work at the paper or going to another college. He admitted that the last one would be difficult for the family. "I do not desire you [miss] the slightest bit of education. I can arrange it, can borrow the money, and we can struggle around without making you feel that you are a burden to anyone. I had to go to work at the very first job I could find and I never had an opportunity to make plans. I do not propose for you to have to do anything of that kind."

In the end, Peyton decided against the surgery and returned home. He received an honorable discharge from the Naval Academy and joined the Naval Reserves. He would have strong ties to the Navy for the remainder of his life.

Back home in Macon, Peyton took his first adult job–in the *Telegraph*'s Merchandising and Servicing Department. Within a few months, he was promoted to Manager of National Advertising.

Kat and Peyton were still in close touch, and when she graduated from Hollins College in 1928, Peyton was ready for marriage. Kat wasn't sure. Instead, she traveled to France, where she planned to study for several months at the Sorbonne in Paris. Peyton was furious. He decided that he wasn't going to wait for her to come back and began dating another girl. In Paris, Kat began seeing a young Scandinavian student. But then she came home for Christmas. They saw each other once and their romance resumed where it had left off.

3

An Acquisition, A Depression, and A Marriage

The *Telegraph* wasn't Macon's only newspaper. For decades the afternoon paper, the *Macon News*, had been the *Telegraph's* fierce competitor. But in 1930 the *News* was in serious trouble. The downward course had begun two years before when the paper endorsed Herbert Hoover, the Republican candidate for president. Georgia was a staunchly Democratic state and angry readers had canceled their subscriptions in droves.

Then the death knell had sounded when the stock market crashed in 1929.

The country was deep in a depression and the future was uncertain, but when R. L. McKenney, owner of the *Macon News*, decided to sell, the Anderson brothers were determined to buy it. The negotiations went forth and eventually an agreement was reached. W. T. and P. T. Anderson would purchase the *Macon News* for a reported $200,000. They planned that the two papers would continue with separate newsrooms and separate editorial staffs. The only publication loss was the Sunday edition of the *News*. The sale was completed on 9 June 1930.

The next day the front page of both papers carried a box containing the following:

ANNOUNCEMENT

Announcement is hereby made that I have this day sold to Mr. W. T. Anderson and Mr. P. T. Anderson, editor and publisher, and general manager, respectively, of The Macon Telegraph, all of my interests, constituting control, of The Macon News Printing Company, and the ownership and management of The Macon News vests in them, beginning with this issue.

I relinquish control of The Macon News after 35 years devoted to its management with the feeling that this newspaper, in the future as in the past, will continue to represent the highest ideals and work for the real welfare of the people of Macon and of this entire community. With the purchase of my stock goes not only the good will, as expressed in terms of law, but my very heartiest best wishes for the progress and prosperity of The Macon News under its new ownership.

I wish to take this opportunity to thank my friends and the public for the cordial cooperation and support they have given me and The Macon News during this period of more than a third of a century in which I have sought to serve them and the city of Macon.

RL McKENNEY
Editor and Publisher

To the Public:

In purchasing the majority stock and taking over the operation of the Macon News Printing Company and the publication of *The Macon News*, we desire to say that it shall be our purpose to eliminate as much as possible the duplicated expenses and use these in improving both newspapers, passing to the public and our patrons the advantage of consolidation.

The policies of the two newspapers will be independent and we rely upon the record of *The Telegraph* as assurance to the public that fair treatment will be accorded in all editorial and news presentations, and that every business transaction shall be characterized by the utmost liberality.

It is our purpose to maintain separate editorial and news staffs, to give these the greatest freedom of opinion and activity in the presentation of views and news, and to endeavor in every way to afford Macon a complete newspaper coverage, in keeping with her growth and importance as a business center.

We expect to abolish the publication of the Sunday edition of The Macon News, as an unnecessary expense and service, and to supply these subscribers, where it is agreeable, with the Sunday Telegraph, with all its additional features, and at no extra cost.

It is our purpose, as soon as details can be worked out to offer a combination subscription rate for both morning and afternoon papers that will be cheaper than heretofore paid by those who took both papers, and to leave it optional with subscribers as to whether they take one or both. The same thing will be worked out for our advertisers, also, although this is not the experience in other cities where combinations of the morning and afternoon papers have been effected.

We beg to assure the public that a sincere effort will be made to make this combination of papers both profitable and satisfactory to everybody, to the end that Macon may get the ultimate and greatest advantage.

MACON TELEGRAPH PUBLISHING COMPANY
W. T. ANDERSON, President
Macon, Ga., June 9, 1930

The same day that announcement appeared in the *Telegraph*, Peyton married Katherine McClure. They'd been engaged only a few months and Peyton's parents were concerned that his youth made him unsuited for marriage at that time, but the two young people were very much in love and determined to marry. Peyton had been promoted to the position of Circulation Manager the previous year and was ready to settle down.

His uncle Eugene wrote Peyton a letter offering advice on the subject of marriage. "There is nothing else in life that means as much to a man. A woman's influence is the greatest power that he can find. She directs him for good or for evil." He also shared his opinion on handling money and marriage. "I hope you can balance your character in such a way that you can get the proper appreciation of money without making it the sole object of existence. Money cannot make married life a success, but the want of it can make married life a failure."

For weeks before their marriage, Kat and Peyton were honored at teas, dinners and parties. Their wedding day was unseasonably cool. Rather than the usual blazing heat of the Macon summer, the high temperatures that week only reached the low eighties and the nights were cool enough to put light blankets on the beds. At 5:30 on the evening of June 10, Peyton and Kat were wed at the First Presbyterian Church in Macon. Kat's uncle, Dr. James McClure, officiated at the service. Five bridesmaids, including Peyton's sister Laura Nelle, attended the bride and her mother was her matron of honor. Peyton chose long-time friend and Riverside Academy classmate Robert Kingsman, Jr., as his best man. The service was followed by a reception at the McClures' Cleveland Avenue home. It was, according to the *Telegraph*, "one of the most interesting and important social events of the week."

The newlyweds moved into the big house on Oakcliff Road with Peyton's parents. They took his bedroom on the second floor at the top of the wide stairs. A small room beside it became their sitting room. Here they had enough space to be comfortable until they found a place of their own. Their wedding gift from P. T. and Nell had been a lot just down the street and the two immediately began planning the sort of home they wanted to build. Peyton continued working with the paper and Kat settled into married life.

Purchasing the *Macon News* had been a great accomplishment, but the timing was terrible. His friends teased P. T. about being R. L. McKenney's Santa Claus. "I don't find that very funny," P. T. would respond when his fellow Kiwanians chided him about the business deal. Even Laura Nelle's friends had some fun at the Andersons' expense. "Have you seen Mr. McKenney's daughters in those good-looking cars?" they'd ask, giggling. "Why don't you have a car?"

Finances were so tight by the end of 1930 that there was speculation that the Andersons would lose both the papers. Their bankers, even newspaper staffers, advised them to get rid of the *News* and cut their losses, but they wouldn't hear of it. Through the loyalty of their employees, the patience of their paper supplier, and the good graces of the Citizens and Southern Bank, they managed to hold on. P. T. used to tell his children, "I want my tombstone to say 'He made 1930.'"

The new year brought no relief from the hard times. In January a mob of angry farmers, their livelihoods destroyed by the ongoing drought, marched on City Hall in England, Arkansas, demanding food for their families. Theirs was only one of many such demonstrations across the nation. The *Telegraph*, never a supporter of Herbert Hoover, published a strong editorial the same week condemning the presidential policies the Andersons believed had led to the problem. It read, in part:

> What [those farmers] wanted was immediate food and they wanted it from businessmen, who, to them represent an economic system that has piled up such enormous surpluses of wheat and sugar and cotton and other commodities that international trade walls and cartels are necessary, but that is not able or intelligent enough to work out any system of distribution that will prevent men and women from starving to death.
>
> Before the farmers of Arkansas staged their march, President Hoover had disapproved the $15,000,000 item in the

drought relief bill on the ground that the Red Cross and other relief agencies were amply able to take care of the situation. Judge John Barton Payne, chairman of the Red Cross, made the same statement. Their estimate has now been revised. Judge Payne has asked Mr. Hoover to appeal for $10,000,000 of public funds to enable the Red Cross to take care of farmers in the belt the drought ravaged.

The Telegraph's personal leaning is toward relief through such agencies as the Red Cross, but that relief will be slow in coming if it is necessary to make a public appeal. We see no good reason whatever why the federal government should not make loans for food for human beings who are the victims of such disasters as droughts. We have appropriated hundreds of millions of dollars for the starving of Belgium and Central Europe and the Far East, but when we are asked to appropriate a paltry sum to the hunger-ridden people of our own nation, we are told that it is Socialistic and a bad precedent and any number of other things.

The thirties were a decade of dark economic times, and the Anderson family was not exempt. Like their neighbors, they had little ready money, but they managed well enough using a kind of bartering system. Local stores advertised in the papers and were often happy to pay for that advertising in goods rather than cash.

Under W. T. Anderson's guidance, the *Macon Telegraph* became a well-respected newspaper. He had a knack for hiring outstanding journalists and allowing them to publish what they chose. A chapter of the American Facisti Association and Order of Blackshirts formed in Atlanta in 1930. It was that organization's announced purpose to keep blacks in the rural areas by taking every possible city job away from them. The *Telegraph* ran a scathing editorial entitled "Crack the Head of This Newest Nasty Thing," denouncing the group.

That editorial brought quick response from around the southeast. The *Norfolk* (Virginia) *Journal and Guide* joined in that denunciation and wrote: "Thanks to the courage and fairness of such able southern editors as W. T. Anderson of the *Macon Telegraph* and Grover C. Hall of the *Montgomery Advertiser*, light is already being turned on the American Facisti Association and Order of the Blackshirts."

The *Independent*, an Atlanta newspaper for black readers, applauded the *Telegraph's* stance in a September 1930 edition. "The *Macon Telegraph* has led the fight in Georgia against the spread of Italian Socialism and Russian Communism and Editor Anderson deserves the support of every liberty loving Georgian in the state, especially the Negroes.

"Let every Negro man in Georgia subscribe for and read the daily *Macon Telegraph* in its patriotic fight to drive communism and fascism out of Georgia."

W. T. had the soul of a crusader and his causes weren't always national or international in scope. In that time of no air conditioning, Macon's citizens routinely sweltered in the steaming summer heat. W. T. refused to make himself even more uncomfortable than the weather was already doing. He refused to wear a coat and tie during hot weather and publicly encouraged others to do the same.

In 1931, Prohibition was in full force. A highway connecting Atlanta and Brunswick was opened for travel and the Macon Junior Chamber of Commerce chose P. T. Anderson as Outstanding Citizen of the Year. A banquet was held in his honor at the City Auditorium.

The same year, Peyton and Kat moved into their new house. It bore little resemblance to the other houses in the neighborhood. It was a small place, built of gray granite from the Andersons' own quarry, and dominated by a very large living room with a huge fireplace. There were two bedrooms, joined by a bath, on one side of the house. A dining room and a kitchen balanced the design on the other side. The front porch that ran the whole width of the structure and the sharply dipping roofline were reminiscent of Kat's Virginia roots.

Peyton and Kat's first child was born on a pleasant, sunny day in early January 1932. They named the baby Katherine McClure Anderson, after her mother. Peyton doted on his new daughter and almost immediately began calling her Little Kat. They hired a young nurse named Emily Bailey to care for the baby during the day. Emily was a charming and efficient young woman and quickly became a favorite with the whole family. P. T., whose grandchildren would call Pops, declared he'd love to be born again and be a child raised by Emily Bailey.

Peyton's branch of Andersons had been in North America for nearly two centuries. An awareness of that history had been passed down through the generations and a family tradition had grown around a plain gold ring that had come into possession of the Andersons in 1765. While sailing from England, one of the early Andersons rescued a young boy from drowning. The boy was one of a set of twins, and the following year his father awarded the hero with a gold ring in which was inscribed the names of the twin boys: "R. Clarke and J. G. Clarke, born Oct. 28, 1754." Since that time, the ring had been passed down from father to son, or, when there was no male heir, to the eldest male kinsman. In August 1932, the ring was given to Peyton Anderson, Jr., by Dr. John R. Anderson. As he presented the ring, Dr. Anderson reminded Peyton that he must give it to his eldest son; or in case he died without one, to the eldest male of the Anderson family.

In 1932, Eugene Anderson ended his association with the Georgia Alabama Business School, but even at age seventy, he wasn't a man inclined to idleness. He began writing feature stories for the *Macon Telegraph*. After a while, the stories evolved into a column called "Around the Circle" that brought readers news from the small towns and rural areas around Macon.

Two years after Eugene returned to the *Telegraph*, another member of the Anderson family joined the staff. Julia Northrop, sister to Eugene, W. T., and P. T., became the paper's first librarian. Her base of operations was a tiny, caged-in office under the skylight that had originally been the telephone center. To reach her, a visitor had to walk up a flight of stairs, through the newsroom and across the catwalk.

Julia Anderson had married William Northrop in Macon some thirty years before. She and William had lived all over the country and he'd had numerous occupations. They'd lived in California and spent a memorable few years in Washington State where they'd kept bees and lived in a tent. She'd been quite happy in her somewhat unconventional marriage, although her family had been skeptical of the match. P. T. was known to say of Northrup, "He could do most anything, but as soon as he was a success, he quit." The couple had been living in Minneapolis when the osteopath for whom Juilia was working closed her practice. W. T. and P. T. offered their sister a job with the *Telegraph* and she took it. She returned to Macon and her husband followed a few weeks later.

Until her arrival on the scene, back issues of the paper were saved by piling them haphazardly in a dusty storeroom. Julia Northrop changed all that. Miss Julia, as the staff learned to call her, was fastidious, particular, and almost frighteningly efficient. While she might have seemed demure when she referred to everyone she worked with as "Mr.," never presuming to use first names, she was a tiger when it came to her job. She developed her own system for keeping and cataloging clippings, and arranged the old papers in such strict order that she could lay her hand on any requested information at a moment's notice. Grown men were afraid to move or remove anything from the library without her permission.

Kat Anderson had a quick, curious mind and numerous interests. One of those was reading. She loved books and was rarely seen without one nearby. Her tastes varied—one day she was deep in a history book, the next she would be reading a popular mystery. In 1936, she began writing a book review column for the *Telegraph*.

Peyton was kept very busy in those years. By 1935, he had been made business manager for both the *Telegraph* and the *News*. He belonged to several civic organizations and continued to serve in the Naval Reserves where he was commissioned as a lieutenant commander. Like his father and uncle before him, Peyton joined the Southern Newspaper Publishers Association and quickly became active in that organization. In 1933, he was elected to a term on the board.

W. T.'s activities kept him in the public eye. He was a member of Rotary, the Elks Club and at one point, president of the Idle Hour Country Club. In 1935 he financed and started the Macon State Market. Through the paper he advocated for soil conservation, crop diversification and better livestock breeding techniques. He also founded the Georgia Banner Ham Association, a farmers' cooperative.

President Roosevelt continued to spend a great deal of his time in Georgia. The main reason, of course, was his ongoing treatment at Warm Springs. However, he also used his visits to do some old-fashioned politicking. In 1935 he spoke at the Georgia Institute of Technology in Atlanta. The following April, he visited Gainesville just days after it was struck by a tornado.

The *Telegraph* had endorsed Franklin Roosevelt's first run for the presidency in 1932. Although he and the President had enjoyed a cordial relationship, W. T. Anderson quickly became disillusioned with the policies of the New Deal. His editorials proclaimed that fact, and in 1936, very much against the wishes of many on his staff, the newspaper endorsed Alf Landon, not Roosevelt, for president. It was the only time in its history that the *Telegraph* had endorsed a Republican candidate for president.

On 31 August 1937, a second daughter was born to Peyton and Kat. She was named Deyerle, which was her maternal grandmother's maiden name. Peyton had been hoping for a boy, but he was immediately entranced by this second beautiful daughter.

He was still quite a young man when his second child was born. His youth, natural excitement and enthusiasm made him a wonderful playmate for his children. He loved to romp in the yard with them and create adventures for them. And, just as he had when he was a boy, Peyton still loved to cook. This worked out well since Kat had never been fond of kitchen chores. She would joke that the only reason she ever wanted to go to the kitchen was to go out the door to her garden on the other side.

An old friend returned to the *Telegraph* on 2 August 1938—a 691-pound, cast pewter eagle. The eagle had originally been hoisted to the top of the old Macon Telegraph Building at Cherry and Second Streets in 1860. There it remained until the newspaper moved to another building at Second and Mulberry in 1882. The newspaper moved a second time in 1911 to 456 Cherry Street. It was to this location that the eagle returned. Joseph W. Clisby, whose father owned the newspaper at the time the gigantic bird was first installed, had it regilded and presented it to W. T. Anderson. It was then affixed to the top of the Telegraph and News Building on Cherry Street, standing guard once more above the newspaper.

In the spring of 1939, Georgia was excited about the prospect of Margaret Mitchell's Pulitzer Prize–winning novel, *Gone With The Wind*, being made into a movie. Clark Gable signed to play Rhett Butler and there had been an international search for the actress to play Scarlett O'Hara. The *Macon Telegraph* pulled off quite a coup when columnist Susan Myrick was hired as a consultant and attended the filming of the blockbuster in Hollywood. She filed weekly accounts of life on the set. Her stories were so popular that they actually boosted the paper's circulation.

4

Preparations for War

Eugene Anderson was left a widower for a second time in 1940. He remarried the following year at age seventy-eight, wedding Sara Phinazee. He continued writing his column, although his brothers were beginning to withdraw from daily participation in the publication of the newspapers. Peyton was ready to move to the next level. He joined with Charles Marsh of the *Austin American Statesman* and Martin Andersen of the *Orlando Sentinel-Star* to form General Newspaper Services. The new company purchased the *Macon Telegraph*, the *Macon News*, and the *Sunday Macon Telegraph and News*. The purchase price, in cash and installment payments, was $1,000,000. Through this arrangement, Marsh and Andersen received two-thirds of the stock and Peyton retained one-third. Peyton was named president of the Telegraph-News Corporation and Floridian Carmage Walls became general manager and publisher.

Peyton enjoyed his new responsibilities and his new position. Kat divided her time between the children, her gardening, and her book reviews. However, in 1940, the editor of the *Telegraph* decided to discontinue her review column. She was disappointed, but soon had reason to smile again. His decision provoked such a protest from readers that it was reversed and Kat was hired to edit a half-page of book reviews for every Sunday edition. The first day the new format appeared in the paper, it was accompanied by a note from Kat herself.

EDITOR'S NOTE: Beginning today, The Telegraph and News present a half-page of book reviews each Sunday. The many letters of protest that arrived after the column was discontinued on the editorial page were most heartening and appreciated.

Thus, with short and to the point reviews, with illustrations and with comment on the new books under the heading MISCELLANY, we venture forth once more in hopes of serving all of you who have faithfully followed this feature in the past and who wish to continue to keep up with what is being published in book form today.

K. M. A.

Some of the reviews were written under her own name, but Kat was not above using several different pseudonyms. She also persuaded friends and acquaintances to contribute their reviews. Roy Rhodenhiser, Jr., and Emtelle M. Clisby were two such contributors. Books were now an even bigger part of Kat's life than they had been before. It was an unusual day when the postman didn't deliver at least one book to the house on Oakcliff Road.

From an early age, Little Kat and Deyerle had the run of the Shirley Hills neighborhood. There weren't a lot of other children around, but they did have a few friends within walking distance in the subdivision. There were woods to explore and they were frequent visitors to their grandparents just up the street. They also spent considerable time with McClures on Cleveland Avenue.

Visiting Peyton at the newspaper was a treat for the girls. They especially loved spending time with Julia Northrop in her tiny office. The librarian might have caused grown men to shake in their shoes, but she had a special regard for children.

For several years, the War Department had been searching for a location to build an army air depot. Several states were in contention and one of the sites being considered was in Middle Georgia. If chosen, it would be an enormous boost to growth all around Macon. Peyton, along with a number of other community leaders, traveled several times to Washington to lobby for the base. Their strongest ally was Georgia Representative Carl Vinson, the same man who had recommended Peyton for the Naval Academy. Vinson arranged for them to meet with senators, congressmen, military leaders, and even the president himself. In the end, the city of Macon sold the War Department a 3,100-acre dairy farm south of the city for one dollar. It turned out to be a very good investment. The depot, which later became the Warner Robins Air Logistics Center, known as Robins Air Force Base, is now the largest industrial complex in the state and has been responsible for the considerable development of the Middle Georgia area.

Europe was in turmoil. Early in 1940, Italy joined Germany in its war against France and Britain. In April, the Nazis invaded and occupied Denmark and Norway. Two months later, German tanks were rolling through Paris and the French surrendered. People in the United States began to believe that America's entry into the war was inevitable.

Peyton Anderson was called to active duty early in 1941 and was assigned to Charleston, South Carolina as Public Relations Officer for the Sixth Naval District. Kat put their house up for rent and started packing. Taking Deyerle to live in a new town was no problem. She was only four years old and would easily adjust to the change. Little Kat, who now insisted on being called Katty, was another matter. Even at nine, she was a strong-minded child and she didn't want to move to Charleston. She had settled into life in the third grade and had a lot of friends she didn't want to leave. Kat and Peyton worried that moving her in the middle of a school year might have an adverse effect on her education. So it was decided that Katty would stay with her McClure grandparents until the end of the school year when she would join her parents and sister.

The Andersons moved into a newly restored, four-story, eighteenth-century townhouse in the historic district of Charleston. Located on the section of East Bay Street that is now called Rainbow Row because the buildings are all painted Caribbean colors, the house fronted right on the sidewalk.

The Andersons spent three years in Charleston. It was a time for raising the awareness of the armed forces and for raising money for the war effort. Film stars and other celebrities made frequent stops in the port city for special events and Peyton often squired them around town. He and Kat were caught up in the busy social swirl of Charleston and she was able to renew friendships with several of her Hollins classmates who lived there.

When the school year ended, Katty rejoined the family in Charleston. Both she and Deyerle loved living in the old house. Their rooms were on the top floor and they relished the fact that their mother didn't get up the stairs all that often to see how neatly they were kept. As in Shirley Hills, the girls were given a lot of independence. In that nearly crime-free time, they were free to wander about Charleston's narrow, cobblestone streets and play on the cannons in Battery Park. In the Fall, both attended school at Ashley Hall.

Because of his position, Peyton had the ear of many influential people, and he used that advantage to benefit folks from home. He was instrumental in getting a number of Macon men commissioned in the Navy, among them Logan Lewis, Ham Napier, Buford Birdsey, and Laura Nelle's fiancé Daniel O'Callaghan. People back in Macon often chuckled at how many Navy officers their little inland town had produced.

Peyton and his family returned home for Laura Nelle's wedding on 9 May 1942. The ceremony at St. Paul's Episcopal Church was quite small. Ten-year-old Katty was Laura Nelle's only attendant. Dan shipped out a week later.

On a warm, rainy night in February 1944, P. T. Anderson died in his Oakcliff Drive home. He was seventy years old and, although he'd suffered from anemia and other ailments for some months, his death was sudden and unexpected.

Peyton and his family made the trip from Charleston for the funeral service at St. Paul's on February 10. *Macon Telegraph* employees made up an honorary escort as the procession traveled from the church to Riverside Cemetery. A tribute to P. T. was run on the editorial page the day he was buried, describing him as "generous, warmhearted, one of those rare spirits who hold their patent of nobility directly from the Creator and go through life with an intuitive sense of when and where they can contribute most to the sum of human happiness."

In the spring, Peyton was detached from the Sixth Naval District and ordered to duty as Public Relations Officer for the Seventh Fleet in the Southwest Pacific. Within days of his notification, he left for Washington, DC, to await traveling orders. Kat and the girls packed their things and, a week later, returned to Macon where they would stay temporarily with her parents. The house on Oakcliff was still occupied by renters and it wouldn't be vacant for several weeks. Knowing a big job lay ahead of her, Kat flew to New York City for a shopping trip and what would probably be her last vacation for quite some time.

As April came to an end, Peyton received his orders. He left DC for San Francisco, but not before sending a telegram to Kat at the Hotel Beekman Towers in New York: "Situation normal miss you terribly. Buy an orchid my love. Peyton."

His flight across the country turned out to be a series of short hops on whatever military transport was available—Washington to Toledo, Chicago, Moline, Omaha, North Platte, Denver, Salt Lake, Denver again, Reno, Sacramento, Oakland and, finally, San Francisco. The several days he spent in San Francisco waiting to make the next leg of the trip were a pleasant respite. He had drinks at the Top of the Mark and dinner at Solaris, but his thoughts remained on his wife. He wrote Kat from there: "Missing you more each minute and can't wait till our reunion. We must keep our chins up and have pride in the days we have spent together. I adore you, I worship you, you're my guiding star."

On May 1, he left San Francisco behind and flew southwest across the vast Pacific, stopping on several islands and eventually landing in Melbourne, Australia. The Navy had arranged quarters for him, as well as other officers and some news correspondents, in the Canberra Hotel. In a letter home, Peyton described his new room as "about the size of our bath with a very uncomfortable bed. It's like a jail cell. I can't help humming The Prisoner's Song every time I enter."

To make matters worse, the hotel was owned and operated by a temperance society. There were three main rules for the guests: no alcohol, no intoxicated people on the premises, and no members of the opposite sex in the rooms. Peyton and the other occupants began referring to the place as The Tower of Virtue.

Soon after arriving in Australia, Peyton learned that his mother, his beloved Mimmie, had suffered a stroke. Even though he was terribly worried about her, he was comforted by the knowledge that Laura Nelle was there with her. The most frustrating aspect of the situation was that he had to rely on the mail for news of his mother's condition. Her improvement, he learned one letter at a time, was slow but steady.

As the days passed, place names like Buna, Moresby, and Hollandia became as familiar to Peyton as Vineville and East Macon. The officers working with him in those early days were Lt. Dick Lundgren, formerly of the Rockford, Illinois, papers, and Lt. Hiller Innis, a photographer who'd been with Paramount Pictures before the war. The unit was responsible for assisting war correspondents in getting the information they needed and setting up meetings between the reporters and those people they wanted to interview. Peyton's specific job was to censor and approve the stories written by the correspondents before they were sent out and to arrange press conferences at General Headquarters for the Seventh Fleet brass. "That will be a job, too," he wrote to Kat, "for I can see the stroke of Doug in minimizing all Naval action. But that's my job and it's made interesting by the battles ahead."

Doug, of course, was Douglas MacArthur. Peyton never had much use for pretense or people who believed they were entitled to special privileges and he was not impressed with the Supreme Commander of the Southwest Pacific. That sentiment was reinforced one morning in June. Peyton had business at Allied Headquarters on Collins Street. He entered a crowded elevator and gave the elderly operator his floor number. The doors started to close, but the operator stopped them at the last minute to allow a tall man in a general's uniform to enter the car.

"Take me to nine," the general barked.

"Yes, sir!"

The doors closed and the car shot upward, stopping on the ninth floor with a stomach lurching halt. There the general got out.

As the doors were closing again, Peyton turned to the operator.

"I asked to get off at five. You didn't stop there. Why take me up to nine first?"

"Why, that was General MacArthur," the operator said reverently.

Peyton could only laugh.

Peyton's letters during that time were full of stories of how he was adjusting to life in Australia. The monetary system was difficult to master, as was driving on the left side of the road. When he was finally able to handle both without a problem, he was proud of the accomplishment. He also made a point of always knowing what time it was in Georgia. Melbourne was fifteen hours ahead of Eastern Standard Time. He had brought P. T.'s watch with him to Australia and it was always set on Macon time.

Peyton wrote to Kat every day, sometimes twice a day. She responded with letters full of news about home and family. However, they were both having trouble keeping up with the order in which the letters had been written. Mail pick-up and delivery in the Pacific was unpredictable. Often they'd receive a more recently written letter days before one that was a week older. Peyton solved the problem by suggesting they number their letters as they were written and the system worked well.

The rules at the Tower of Virtue didn't remain intact for very long. Most of the men began keeping bottles of whiskey in their rooms. Peyton did so as well and fell into a daily habit of having a drink "with Kat" before dinner every night. He'd pour a splash of bourbon into a glass and, standing in front of her picture, would toast her and drink it, pretending she was there with him.

Back in Macon, the Andersons were settling into a routine without Peyton. They'd moved back into their house and Kat was in the early stages of redecorating the place. She had a talent for interior design and the work kept her busy. She'd also resumed writing book reviews for the *Telegraph*. Katty and Deyerle had both entered Alexander III Elementary School and neither girl showed any ill effects from the move. But Deyerle was sick for much of May and June. She had a two-week bout with measles and, almost immediately afterwards, contracted mumps. Kat wrote to Peyton and passed on what Deyerle had had to say about her run of bad luck. "Well, I'll get everything over at one time," she'd told her mother. Her father was proud of the philosophical way she faced the situation.

5

In the Pacific

A million Allied troops moved onto the Normandy beaches on 6
June 1944 and began the major European offensive. On the
other side of the world, there was intense speculation as to when the
Allies would start their push north in the Pacific. Everyone believed
it had to be very soon. Peyton drew his combat gear: .45 automatic,
holster, canteen, cup and cover, mess kit, flashlight, mosquito
netting, socks, shoes, gloves, and sun helmet. Two days later, he got a
preview of what lay ahead when he was invited along on a
reconnaissance flight over New Guinea. They took off in a driving
rainstorm just before dawn, flew most of the day and spent the night
in a Quonset hut in Port Moresby. The next day, they "crossed the
hump," flying over 5,000-foot Mt. Wilhelm, and then visited the
islands off the north coast. The same day that they returned to
Australia, American B-29 bombers conducted the first raid on the
Japanese mainland.

Father's Day was approaching and Katty wrote her father to tell
him about his present. "Dear Peyton," she wrote—both of his
children called him by his first name, most often shortening it to
Pate. "Now days it's so hard to get something nice. Usually I get
something just for you. This year I got something for all of us. With
the money I was going to spend on a present for you, I bought
enough stamps to fill out my book and buy a bond. See, it's

something for all of us. Something to bring you home faster. I hope this is all right with you."

Peyton was touched. He responded with thanks, saying that she had inspired him to purchase two more bonds, one in her name and one in Deyerle's.

Soon afterwards, Deyerle put her thoughts on paper as well. She wrote that she missed him and wanted him to come home because he was "so much fun". Her letter delighted him. The next time he wrote to Kat, he declared that he couldn't think of anything he'd rather have his children say about him.

July brought significant progress in the war in the Pacific. Guam was liberated and Allied forces secured Saipan. Near the end of the month Peyton took another flying tour of New Guinea. This one lasted fourteen days. It was an exhausting two weeks of bumpy rides, discomfort, and little sleep. On their way back to Australia they stopped for fuel at Milne Bay and picked up some surprise passengers—comedian Jack Benny and a troop of other USO entertainers. They were a lively group, full of jokes and stories of their travels, and their presence made the rest of the trip almost enjoyable.

The move north was now imminent. By August 28, Peyton was packing up his office and getting ready to leave Australia for good. He sent Kat a change of address—Staff, Commander 7th Fleet, Advanced Headquarters—and told her he'd also written her another letter "in case something should happen to me, but you won't get it until I deliver it in person cause, Baby darling, I am acoming back to you."

Within a week, Peyton and his staff were settling into their new base in the highlands of New Guinea. It was quite a change from their urban Australian accommodations. The Tower of Virtue had been left far behind. Now they lived and worked in Quonset huts with only cold-water showers and canned food. It was an inconvenient and uncomfortable location, but not especially dangerous. "Please understand I am on a mountain in a place the Japs haven't bothered to raid in four months," he wrote home, "sitting up with lights ablaze and everything brighter than Broadway in peacetime."

Peyton's level of comfort improved greatly a month later when Admiral Thomas Kinkaid had him moved into a cabin on his own flagship. This was done so that the Public Relations Officer would be on hand to assist the reporters on board during the upcoming battle. A few days later, the Allies landed in the Philippines.

When they took the beach at Leyte, Peyton found himself in the middle of a firefight. He'd gone ashore shortly after the landing to get information for the correspondents. He described the situation to Kat in a letter he wrote that night: "I went ashore to find Colonel Diller. Found him in a foxhole. I asked him questions while a few bullets whizzed overhead." He wasn't hurt even though the enemy was scattered in pillboxes only 150 yards away. And he couldn't help feeling proud of one thing. "After all, I landed on a Philippines beach—the most bitterly contested, too, within two hours of the time the first troops hit it—and, by the way, AHEAD of General MacArthur."

Although he left the Leyte beach unscathed, Peyton was injured a few days later attempting to step into a small boat that had come alongside of the flagship. An unexpected wave caused him to lose his footing and he severely sprained his knee—the same knee he'd injured sixteen years before at Annapolis. He was incapacitated for days and limped about for weeks afterwards.

December was unusually cold in Georgia that year and snow fell as far south as Macon. Kat tried to keep busy working on the house, but as the holidays drew near her thoughts turned more and more to her absent husband. She felt overwhelmed sometimes, caring for the children, and overseeing the upkeep on the house and the vehicles. Katty and Deyerle were doing well. In fact, Katty had made the honor roll at her school. But Kat missed Peyton and longed to share her life with him again.

Of course, Christmas was a difficult time for all families, as well as the servicemen who were so far away from home. Peyton had an additional reason for sadness that year. It was the first Christmas since P. T.'s death. "Tomorrow would have been Dad's birthday," he wrote on December 20. "If he was alive, there'd have been the big party."

Peyton left the flagship in December and he and his unit were moved to a Quonset hut in Hollandia, New Guinea. A familiar face joined the staff there. Lt. Cloud Morgan, who had worked at the radio station WMAZ in Macon, came on board as a radioman. He'd been stationed in Australia in 1944 and gotten engaged to a local girl named Joyce Lang. He wrote to his old friends at WMAZ about his approaching marriage and they sent the letter over to the *Telegraph*, where it was published. Peyton regularly received copies of the paper. When he saw the letter, he immediately wrote to Morgan in Australia, asking if he would consider joining the Seventh Fleet Public Relations staff. Morgan was a young man who was eager to get into the war. Even though it meant leaving his new bride, he wrote Peyton that he wanted to go. He reported to Hollandia in January 1945.

On January 6, the fleet was on the move again and Peyton was back on Kinkaid's flagship. This time they were en route to the Lingayen Gulf on the west coast of the Philippine island of Luzon, 107 miles from Manila. The ship was unusually quiet the night before the landing. Everyone who could had been asleep by 9:30 in anticipation of the pre-dawn invasion, but Peyton, his staff and the few correspondents aboard were wide awake. The newsmen were hurriedly writing articles to be filed the next morning. Peyton lay in his bunk until the early hours, reading, censoring, and approving them.

By the 11th, the invasion was accomplished and the area secure enough that Peyton was able to go ashore with some of the reporters to have a look around Luzon. A couple of days later, they took a trip up the Dagupan River to the city of the same name. There they mingled with the citizens—many of whom had recently returned from the hills where they had hidden for years from the Japanese occupation forces. They also met the former mayor of the town, toured the cathedral, and then walked around seeing the sights.

It was on this walk that they passed a house that had been newly acquired as quarters for General MacArthur. The Supreme Commander himself was in a rocking chair on the porch. To Peyton's surprise, he greeted the group, invited them in, and allowed himself to be interviewed by the correspondents. He was relaxed and hospitable, lacking the formality Peyton had grown used to seeing during his time in Australia.

While Peyton knew his primary function was facilitating the activities of the war correspondents and issuing press releases for the fleet, he came up with another program he believed would benefit the Navy and the people back in the US. He wanted to send his own staff around the fleet to interview servicemen, get their stories on recorders, and send them back to the States for play on their hometown radio stations.

Somehow, Peyton acquired six wire recorders—the precursors of tape recorders. They were the first in the Navy and Peyton put Cloud Morgan to work training the rest of the staff to use them. Twenty three-minute interviews could be recorded on one spool of wire, which was then sent back to Washington, transcribed onto phonograph records and sent out to the various radio stations. After a short time, Morgan and his trainees were sending several hundred recordings a week to Washington.

Once more, Peyton left the ship for land and was assigned to a large Quonset hut with a number of other men. It was not an arrangement he enjoyed and he said so in a letter to Kat: "I am really plum tired of this 'prep school' life. Living with no privacy in a space not as big as our living room with 12 other people and carrying on just like school boys."

In February, the Marines began the month-long battle for Iwo Jima. The next month the American flag was raised over Corregidor and US bombers launched incendiary bomb attacks against Tokyo. Easter Sunday brought the news that the American assault on Okinawa had begun. The war finally seemed to be going America's way and there was cautious optimism in the ranks. Then, on April 14, they got shocking news.

The early risers in the hut were up at 6:00 A.M. and sat around, chatting and drinking coffee as usual. Peyton had turned his radio on low for some music when Hugh McLauren, the base medical officer, suddenly jumped to his feet and rushed across the room to turn up the radio.

"My ears must be failing me or I just heard the President was dead," he shouted.

Of course, he was right. Franklin Delano Roosevelt, the thirty-second president of the United States, had died the day before of a cerebral hemorrhage in Warm Springs, Georgia. All conversation in the hut stopped, its occupants mute with disbelief.

Just across the way was the hut occupied by Marine Colonel James Roosevelt, son of the president. Only minutes before, they'd heard him burst into song, as was his habit when rising in the morning. But the song stopped abruptly in mid-word. They realized that he, too, must have had his radio on.

A hush gradually fell over the camp as the news spread. Even those people who hadn't been admirers of the President's policies were saddened at the death of their commander and chief. People began pouring into Jimmy Roosevelt's hut to express their sympathy. Others worried that this one man's death would change the direction of the war.

"We have lost a great leader," Peyton wrote to Kat. "I am not concerned about the future. We as a country are too big to be set back by the loss of any one man. Though I feel it would take less bickering if he were there in post war plans. Truman, a man I shall never forget having met in Charleston and believe to be honest, sincere and not easily fooled, should be a good man to fill his shoes."

As the war continued to wind down, Peyton's thoughts turned more and more to life after the military and the role he would play when he returned to civilian life. He shared his concerns in a letter to his wife: "I cannot be satisfied to be just 'junior' as I have all my life in Macon. I don't like being famous for being someone's son, someone's nephew. But I doubt if that will be easy in Macon with Mr. W. T. there. It will require a lot of moving around. I believe I know how to do it—my first effort will be to become known as myself, so we'll have a lot of traveling around the state and I'll have to arise from a member of the audience to a noisy guy. I don't mean a show off, but to let people know I'm alive with a mind of my own. I have lost all fear of talking to a crowd. I believe I have things to talk about, so here I go."

Germany's surrender on May 8 set off a round of celebrations among the troops in the Pacific. Now it seemed certain that the end was in sight for all of them. Peyton started off early in the day on the beach in the company of an Australian Royal Air Force lieutenant and a bottle of scotch. As the hours passed, he moved on to other parties in other places. It was a day of abandon, hilarity and deep relief that the war in Europe was over.

While he'd been in the service, Peyton had kept in touch with Charles Marsh and Martin Andersen, as well as Carmage Walls. In November 1944, Martin wrote to tell him that General Newspapers, the company that owned the *Macon Telegraph and News*, had made a bid for *The Augusta Chronicle*, *The Columbus Record*, and the Spartanburg, South Carolina, papers. As it turned out, their bid was unsuccessful, but it was clear that they were looking to expand the company and Peyton was eager to be a part of it. Within another year, they would try again and succeed in purchasing *The Spartanburg Herald and Journal.*

Another change took place in Peyton's absence. Charles Marsh bought out Martin Andersen's interest in the *Macon Telegraph and News*. Peyton was not satisfied with the resulting arrangement—Marsh now owned two-thirds of the stock and he owned only one-third. He hoped that Marsh would be willing to work with him when he got back and sell him more of the stock so that they'd each own half of the company. It was on the top of his list of things to do as soon as he got back home.

In May, Peyton learned that Robert Manigault, owner of the Charleston newspapers, was very ill and not expected to live. He wrote to Kat and, after expressing sympathy for the man, wondered if the family might be interested in selling the papers if and when the owner died.

Shortly after receiving Peyton's letter, Kat attended an art exhibit. There she learned that Robert Manigault had died. Kat was a resourceful woman who saw a great opportunity before her. That night she could hardly sleep, contemplating the possibility of purchasing the Charleston papers she knew Peyton desperately wanted to own. By nine o'clock the next morning, she was on the phone to Charles Marsh with the news. He immediately went to work. Two hours later, he called her back with the news that he could raise a million dollars for the deal, but hadn't been able to get any definite information by telephone about the Manigault family's intentions. Kat decided to go to Charleston herself and see what she could find out.

She flew up the next day. Using the social connections she'd made when she and Peyton were stationed there, she inquired into the status of the ownership of the newspapers and let it be known that General Newspapers was interested in talking about a sale. In the end the Manigault family decided to retain ownership of the newspapers. But that development didn't keep Peyton from being proud of Kat's work on his behalf.

"You did wonderful in Charleston as I knew you would," he wrote to her. "I have read, reread and read your letter and am especially impressed with the manner you approached the situation and how tactfully you handled it."

In June, Peyton's title was changed from Public Relations Officer to Public Information Officer, and in August he was promoted to full Commander. But those personal victories were overshadowed by the events taking place in the Pacific. On August 6, the first atomic bomb ever used in warfare was dropped on Hiroshima, Japan. Three days later, Nagasaki fell to the same fate.

Peyton wrote to Kat, "The news of the new atomic bomb has us all speculating. It seems to be a discovery of how civilization can destroy itself. A horrible weapon, but just what is needed to end the Japanese planned eternal aggression. This thing, if as great as is pictured, should be the necessary weapon to bring about an end of all wars."

Less than a week later, Japanese Emperor Hirohito announced, "We cannot continue the war any longer." Japan accepted the Allies' conditions for surrender.

Although the formal surrender would not take place until September 2, the war was for all practical purposes over and attention turned to the practicalities of the end of hostilities. Arrangements for the formal surrender and return of prisoners of war had to be made. In pursuit of that, several high-ranking officials from Japan traveled to the Philippines to meet with Allied commanders. Peyton was on hand on August 19 to welcome the Japanese emissaries and escort them to the meetings.

"Here I go getting in on history," he wrote Kat, "but it's all in a day's work."

The third week of August, Cloud Morgan left New Guinea for Australia. Having served over two years in the Pacific, he was entitled to be rotated back home for thirty days and he wanted to take his wife with him. The only problem was that the ships carrying the wives and children of US servicemen back to the States—known as bride ships—were always crowded and the waiting lists were long. Since they'd married late in the war, Morgan's wife had a low priority for transportation to the US. But if a serviceman were present when the ship docked, he was assured of a place in line ahead of any non-military personnel. And, in that event, he could take his wife with him. Peyton promised that when they learned of a ship scheduled to stop at Australia and pick up brides, he'd see to it that Morgan got his orders back to the states at the same time.

"Only thing you'll have to do is find your own transportation back to Australia."

Morgan knew that wouldn't be difficult. The Air Force and Navy pilots made frequent runs down to Australia to pick up liquor and bring it back to the Philippines. So he hitched a ride with one of them early one morning. That night he and Joyce boarded a ship together.

Morgan wasn't the only one returning to the States. By the end of August, the war was over for Peyton Anderson. He'd been given a thirty-day leave and transferred back to the United States. When the Japanese formally surrendered to General MacArthur on 2 September 1945, in Tokyo Bay, Peyton was home with his family in Macon.

6

Post-War Macon

The girls were elated to have their father home and Peyton and Kat enjoyed a wonderful reunion. They danced at the club, saw the new Joan Crawford movie, and spent hours and hours talking. Best of all from his point of view, Peyton slept in his own bed in his own house. When his leave was over on October 4, he flew to Charleston and reported to the Naval Separation Center. There he went through the necessary processing to be placed on inactive duty status. Days later, he was on his way back home to resume his life as a civilian.

General Newspapers also owned the *Gadsden* (Alabama) *Times*. Shortly after his return home, Peyton was named general manager of that paper while still maintaining his position as president of the Macon Telegraph Publishing Company. His new responsibilities required him to spend a great deal of time in Gadsden, but he didn't move his family to Alabama. They'd been moved around enough, he believed, and didn't need any more turmoil in their lives. Kat and the girls were happily settled in Macon, close to friends and family. Laura Nelle and her husband Dan had moved into the big Anderson house across the street to be near Nell Anderson, whose health was still far from good. Deyerle was at Alexander III Elementary School and Katty at Lanier Junior High, and both were doing well in their studies.

So Peyton commuted back and forth a couple of times a week to Alabama. It was a less-than-ideal situation. He was tired a lot of the time and he missed many of the girls' activities. Occasionally, they'd talk about a move to Gadsden, but each time, Kat and Peyton would decide against it.

In his later years, Peyton had quite a reputation for finding and developing new talent. It was a knack he discovered early in his career. During his first days as general manager of *The Gadsden Times*, he attended a cocktail party to get acquainted with the employees. A young reporter named Ruth Hagedorn was chatting with him over the hors d'oeuvres and said off-handedly, "I've always wanted to write a column." This comment had always brought laughter from his predecessor, but not from Peyton.

"Go ahead. Write me five columns and we'll see."

Ruth did as he asked, working and reworking the columns until she decided they were ready. Then she nervously presented them to Peyton. He read her work and, without further discussion, made her a columnist for the paper. She was an immediate success with the readers. That one conversation began a career that lasted over forty years.

On a warm November night in 1945, W. T. Anderson died at his home in Shirley Hills after a two-month bout with leukemia. W. T. had been a great influence on the city and was loved by many of its citizens. Peyton wrote a glowing memorial to his uncle that appeared on the front page of the *Telegraph*. The funeral service was held at the First Presbyterian Church and W. T. was buried beside his wife in Rose Hill Cemetery.

Peyton Anderson was active in the Macon Chamber of Commerce and helped plan a gala celebration at the Hotel Dempsey in April 1946 to honor Fleet Admiral Chester W. Nimitz. Carmage

Walls, president of General Newspapers, was retiring as president of the Chamber and was also being recognized for his service.

The biggest surprise of the evening came when Admiral Nimitz, during an intermission of the dinner program, awarded the Bronze Star to Peyton Anderson for "meritorious conduct as a member of the Staff of Commander Seventh Fleet from May 4, 1944 to August 15, 1945." The citation, signed by Admiral Kinkaid, praised Peyton's "resourceful initiative, excellent administrative ability and unceasing efforts to obtain complete and outstanding news and photographic coverage of Seventh Fleet activities." It continued, "He participated in the initial phases of the Naval operations at Sansapor, Dutch New Guinea, Leyte and Lingayen Gulf in the Philippines displaying outstanding coolness and efficiency under fire, in placing war correspondents and combat photographers in order to obtain maximum news coverage of the action."

A second award was made that evening. James H. Porter, a local business leader and gardener, presented Admiral Nimitz with a new double-flowering camellia. The bright red blossom had been named the Admiral Nimitz Camellia.

General Newspapers experienced a shake up the following year. Peyton replaced Phil Buchheit as publisher of the *Macon Telegraph and News*. Buchheit moved to Spartanburg, South Carolina, and Carmage Walls, then president of General Newspapers, went to Gadsden, Alabama. Bert Struby, who had worked as a reporter for the Macon paper before going into the military, was named executive editor of the *Telegraph and News*.

Peyton continued his membership with the Southern Newspaper Publishers Association and, later that year, was reelected to the board of directors. In addition to important business contacts, the SNPA provided Peyton and Kat with a reason to travel. Each spring they went to New York for the American Newspaper Publishers Association convention and to New Orleans for the SNPA annual meeting. As soon as the girls were old enough, they were included.

Not all their travel was related to business. Peyton was an enthusiastic hunter and fisherman and, more often than not, Katherine went right along with him. She was game to try anything and once shot two birds with one bullet. The girls accompanied them on these trips as well. Their father was very patient teaching them to cast a fishing rod or shoot a gun.

Peyton was often spontaneous. One Christmas Day, after the presents had been opened and the meal eaten, he made a suggestion.

"Let's go to Florida!"

They piled in the car and headed south to Boca Grande, making it just in time to catch the last ferry to the island. Fishing in Florida became something of a Christmas tradition and the four of them often made the trip after the festivities in Macon were over.

When Kat could persuade him, the family would travel overseas and visit historical places. But Peyton didn't feel wonder at the sight of architectural accomplishments from other ages. "I hate going to these places," he'd tell his daughters, "because all I see is one group of people or one family being enormously wealthy at the great expense of thousands of people that were doing without. You mother sees something different, but I don't like it. It influences me so that I don't appreciate what I'm seeing."

That opinion was representative of how Peyton viewed the world as a whole. He wanted people be treated with kindness and respect. He had great concern for his community and realized that his and his family's prosperity was tied to the prosperity of that community. He wouldn't hear of anyone in his household shopping in Atlanta. More than once, Peyton told his children, "The money I have is not mine. It's not mine because this money was made in the community and it was made because the community flourished. Therefore I was able to flourish and this money rightfully should go back to the well being of the community."

In Peyton's eyes, the worst sin his children could commit was being rude or not treating all people equally. He never referred to anyone who worked at the house as a servant nor did he ever say anyone at the paper worked *for* him. In Peyton's world people worked together or one person helped another.

Once Deyerle went to her father, concerned because one of the men who worked at their house had stolen a small item. "Oh, yes," Peyton said. "But he's fine. He's just a petty thief." He spoke as if he understood the man's capabilities and his problems and accepted both. No more was said about it and the man continued to work there.

Peyton did his best to instill his philosophy in his children. Over and over, he'd preach, "Don't let a jackass set your standards for you." That line was enough to stop any argument that "everybody else is doing it."

He also taught them, by example, the best ways to deal with other people. Peyton didn't like conflict and he didn't like bullies. He emphasized that, in any situation, you had to consider the other person's reactions to what happened. It was important to let them keep their pride. "Don't push me into a corner," he advised. "Give me a way out. If you push me in a corner, I can't acquiesce. Give me a way out." His children listened and remembered.

The Andersons employed a cook but that didn't keep Peyton out of the kitchen, especially when he and Kat entertained. Blanche and David Redding were frequent guests, as were Bob and Margena Dunlap. An invitation for drinks often progressed to an impromptu dinner put together by Peyton and Kat.

Peyton's cooking wasn't just reserved for company. Steaks, short ribs, dove, and quail were all favorites that he made for his family. He was not, however, fond of vegetables. It was usually up to Kat to put together a salad or find another green accompaniment to Peyton's meals. One of the dishes he most enjoyed preparing was spaghetti, perhaps because it was Deyerle's favorite. His sauces would simmer on the stove for hours. He even found a little Italian grocery store near St. Joseph's Catholic Church where he could buy fresh pasta.

Shopping was another of his pleasures. He wasn't one to run into a grocery store to pick up a loaf of bread and a quart of milk. The girls loved going with him because he made shopping an adventure. His favorite place in the store was the meat department, where he'd talk at length with the butcher. After a few minutes, he'd be behind the counter, Katty and Deyerle at his heels. Then they'd all go back into the meat lockers and the butcher would show them what he had, sometimes cutting off a piece of meat right there and letting Peyton taste it. Then the selection would be made.

Peyton would go up and down the aisles loading up his cart, all the while talking to the employees. He showed them great respect, asking their advice and praising their expertise. When he finally made his way out of the store, laden with food, nearly everyone who worked there trailed along behind him, thanking him for his business and telling him to come back soon.

When Katty was fifteen or sixteen years old, she took a summer job in the circulation department at the newspaper. She spent most of that summer answering the telephone and assuring people whose papers had not been delivered that they would be sent out immediately. The next year she worked as an assistant to Jeannette Gausch, her father's secretary. But two summers' exposure couldn't convince her that the newspaper business was in her future. As she said later, "I wasn't Katharine Graham." That was the last time she ever worked for a newspaper.

Helping people came naturally to Peyton Anderson. He was interested in the folks he knew and what was happening in their lives. He often strolled through the Telegraph Building, visiting the composing room, the newsroom, and the pressroom, talking with employees, asking about their families and soliciting their concerns. That interest made a real difference in the life of one young woman.

In 1947, Del Ward graduated from Breneau College in Gainesville, Georgia, with a degree in history and the expectation of a career teaching school. That was what was expected of a young woman at the time. When she returned home to Macon, she went right down to the Board of Education to find out what she had to do to start teaching in the fall. With that arranged, she looked around for a part-time job to keep her busy during the summer.

Del's father Ruben Ward, known as Red, was the pressroom foreman at the newspaper. He had worked for the *Macon Telegraph* for over twenty years and had known Peyton Anderson at least that long. One June evening Red came home with a suggestion for his daughter.

"I saw Peyton Anderson today and he asked about you, wanted to know what you were doing. I told him you were looking for a summertime job and he said to tell you to call the radio station."

The paper had recently acquired a part-interest in local radio station WNEX. When he heard that Del Ward needed a job, Peyton called the station and put in a good word for her. The next morning she went down for an interview. To her surprise, she was hired on the spot as a receptionist. More exciting than that, they also allowed her do a daily radio program. That job began a long, successful career. Del never taught school. She went from Macon to WGN in Chicago, then on to New York. She finally returned to Macon for a career in television that is still going strong today.

Nell Anderson never completely recovered from the stroke she had in 1944. She lived the next four years as a semi-invalid. Then in 1948, she contracted pneumonia and died at her home on Tuesday night, November 16. Her funeral was at St. Paul's and she was buried beside P. T. in Riverside Cemetery. That morning the lead editorial in the *Macon Telegraph* was entitled "In Tribute to Mrs. P. T. Anderson, Sr." and described her as "all that is best in wifehood, motherhood and community activities."

7

Family, Friends, and Employees

As the fifties dawned, the baby boom was on. National politics was full of the communist threat and hydrogen bomb tests. School children learned to duck and cover and, after more than a decade of world consciousness, Americans were turning their attention back to their own country.

The house at 1182 Oakcliff Road had started its life as a small structure. When their children were born, Peyton and Kat added a couple more rooms onto the house, but they'd always wanted to do more. It was something they'd talked about for years and was the subject of many wartime letters. In 1950, the time had come to act on those dreams. They added a new kitchen and a dining room. The kitchen was Peyton's own design—very large with every kind of cooking paraphernalia imaginable, and furnished with comfortable chairs so that people could sit in the kitchen with him while he cooked.

Some of the happiest times in his life were spent in that kitchen. He prepared countless meals there and, when cake mixes in boxes began appearing on grocery store shelves, Peyton expanded his repertoire to include baking. It was a challenge he was determined to master. He spent hours baking cakes until he was satisfied with the results. Angel food cake eventually emerged as his favorite.

Peyton never lost his fascination for tinkering. He'd spend hours repairing a $10 item rather than buy a new one. He especially enjoyed wiring projects and sometimes enlisted Deyerle's help. It wasn't unusual for him to have her crawling around under the house, pulling wires to be poked up through the floor at various places. He wired the house for burglar alarms as well as audio speakers. His music system, purchased one component at a time, was large and complicated, so much so that his wife and children were afraid to touch it.

His tinkering wasn't confined to his own home. A quick visit to his sister could result in his tackling a full-blown project. He repaired the furnace, fixed lamps, and installed appliances in Laura Nelle's house. Once when she was having some changes made in a room, Peyton dropped by to see it. He looked around and then his eye focused on the thermostat, which had been relocated.

"That ought not to be up there," he said.

"I know," Nelle answered with a sigh. She agreed that it was an awkward place for the thermostat, but it wasn't a big enough problem to warrant calling back the contractor.

"Wait a minute," Peyton said. He went out to his car and returned with a few tools. Half an hour later the thermostat had been moved to a better location.

The *Macon Telegraph and News* were gaining reputations as independent, creative publications. Beginning in the mid-forties, the two papers had gradually pulled away from Georgia's Talmadge-dominated political machine. While the papers operated independently, they did join together to oppose the election of Herman Talmadge for governor. This wayward behavior prompted Talmadge to refer to the Macon papers as a "carpet-bagging…foreign-owned" press. They weren't, of course, foreign-owned, although General Newspapers, a corporation which now owned six southern papers, didn't own any Georgia papers except the *Telegraph and News*.

Peyton had grown up thinking of the *Telegraph and News* as his family's newspapers and had never been really comfortable that a large block of the stock belonged to General Newspapers. Backed by the financial support of the Jefferson Standard Insurance Company of North Carolina, Peyton bought out General Newspapers on 3 January 1951, and retired the stock. He also purchased Drinnon Photography and made that a part of the Macon Newspapers family. The next day, the front page of the *Telegraph* carried the headline "Peyton Anderson Acquires Control of The Macon Telegraph And News." The accompanying story traced Peyton's history with the paper and contained his statement concerning the sale.

> It has always been my ambition to own the *Macon Telegraph* and the *Macon News*. This dream is today becoming a reality by the acquisition of the stock formerly owned by General Newspapers, Inc. This transaction has been made possible by the confidence and support of the people of Macon and Middle Georgia. I appreciate their loyalty and devotion to these newspapers.
>
> I fully realize the responsibility the acquisition of the papers puts upon me. I feel I am capable of meeting the task. The papers' most valuable asset is a great tradition of honesty, fairness, tolerance and courage. This shall be preserved and serve as an example for each of us in giving to Macon and to Georgia even better newspapers.
>
> No personnel changes are anticipated. Our associates are well qualified. They are equal to the tasks assigned to them.

Soon after Peyton purchased it, the *Macon Telegraph* observed its 125th birthday, and letters of congratulation poured in from all over the country. President Harry Truman, Senator Richard Russell, Senator Walter F. George, Congressman Carl Vinson, and even Governor Herman Talmadge sent their best wishes.

US Representative Carl Vinson, who had been so instrumental in getting Robins Air Force Base located in Middle Georgia, had been a good friend to the Anderson family over the years. So when

Peyton learned that Vinson was going to fly in an airplane for the first time in his life, he went to Robins Air Force Base to meet him. Vinson landed, none the worse for his new experience, and brought with him a popular senator from Texas. It was not the first time Peyton had met Lyndon Johnson. He and Kat had had that pleasure some months earlier while visiting Washington, DC.

Henry Prentiss Smith was named for the doctor who delivered him and was always called Doc. When he was nine years old in 1908, he started delivering papers for the *Macon Telegraph*. From then until he retired at age sixty-five, he worked for the newspaper. He and his wife Vera had two daughters—Berma and Dorothy. Berma graduated from college in 1946 and taught school for three years in Macon, but she was an adventurous young woman and wanted to see something of the world. She joined the Special Services, a governmental organization that set up shop wherever US servicemen were stationed to improve moral and provide on-base entertainment.

Soon after joining, Berma was sent to Germany where she worked in a servicemen's club on a military base. It was the mission of Special Services to provide comfortable surroundings where servicemen could go and relax or read or play cards or board games. The young women employees were there for company and conversation. They planned dances, birthday parties, and hayrides to entertain the soldiers and keep them on the post and out of trouble.

It was in this capacity that Berma met John Ramfjiord. There was an instant attraction and, in 1950, the two were married. They took their vows in a civil service in a nearby town. Such a thing was strictly forbidden and John and Berma had to hide their marriage. They couldn't openly proclaim their marriage and they certainly couldn't live together. Berma had a small apartment in town and John lived on the base.

Although the US Army didn't know about their change in status, Berma couldn't keep the exciting news from her parents. She called home and told them all about the marriage and the situation in which she found herself. Because Special Services girls weren't allowed to marry, she explained, she would have to return home alone and wait until John was assigned somewhere that she could join him.

Doc and Vera were concerned because their daughter was unhappy and Doc mentioned it to Peyton. He expected only a sympathetic ear, but Peyton Anderson was a man accustomed to solving problems. His first impulse was to call Congressman Carl Vinson. Vinson chaired the House Armed Services Committee and Peyton hoped he could do something for the young couple. Although his intention was only to help this time Peyton's intercession was not the best thing for everyone concerned.

Across the Atlantic, Berma got a telephone call at her apartment.

"Is this Mrs. Ramfjiord?" the caller asked.

She hesitated a moment, since her marriage was supposed to be a secret, but then answered with the truth. "Yes, it is."

He introduced himself as an Army sergeant on the base there in Germany. They had, he said, gotten a cablegram from Congressman Vinson wanting to know why she had to come home and offering to help with the situation.

Berma was astonished. "I don't know anything about that."

Then the sergeant asked, "Ma'am, may I ask you something? Is your husband going to stay in the service?"

"Yes, he's a career soldier."

"Well, ma'am, if you take this offer of help, your husband's personnel file will be pulled out and a red "PI" will be stamped in the middle of it, which means political influence. He will never, ever get a promotion or decent post again. That's it. He'll be finished in the service."

Berma took a deep breath. "Could you get me on the first ship or plane home? I'll leave today if you want me to."

He said leaving right then wouldn't be necessary, but that he would arrange for her transport back to the States within the next few days.

Berma left Germany three days later and cried all the way home.

But the young couple wasn't separated for long. She was able to join him a few months later. They were stationed in several different places before ending up in Hawaii in the mid-fifties. When Peyton found out about their posting there, he tried once more to do something for Doc and Vera, and this time he was successful. He gave the Smiths a trip to Hawaii where they were able to spend two weeks with John and Berma.

Peyton loved children and buying them presents gave him great happiness. When they were young, his own daughters were the chief beneficiaries of this generosity, but after they were grown, he turned his attention to the other little ones in the family. He was always on hand every Christmas Eve to help his cousins assemble toys for their children. Laura Nelle's and Dan's daughter Denny, born in 1949, became one of his favorites. He gave her her first bicycle, complete with training wheels, and taught her to ride it in her driveway. Her dog Butch was also a present from her uncle.

Denny didn't care much for dolls and one year announced she wanted an electric train set for Christmas. Nothing could have pleased Peyton more. He bought the nicest one he could find. Then, on a huge piece of plywood, he built a town—houses, stations, trees, crossings—through which the train could run. It was a fine Christmas present. When Denny began showing a fondness for sports, Peyton made sure she had golf clubs and archery equipment.

The *Telegraph and News* was known for hiring promising young journalists. In late 1951, Jim Chapman went to work for the *Telegraph*. He was a World War II veteran and a recent graduate of Emory University. He and his wife Nancy had both grown up in Jacksonville, and Jim was looking for a position with a big city paper. Jobs weren't easy to come by, though, and when a friend told him of an opening for a reporter on the Macon paper, Chapman applied for it and got the job.

He was impressed with Peyton Anderson from their first meeting. "He had that bearing of a Navy commander," he said later. "That ramrod straight posture. But even with that military bearing, there was a side of Peyton that was almost fatherly as far as his employees were concerned." Although Jim and Nancy didn't plan to stay very long, Macon quickly became home for them. Chapman would go on to work in a number of positions with the *Telegraph* before retiring in 1990.

A second young reporter began working for the *Telegraph* in 1951. Reg Murphy was a part-time sports stringer for the paper while he was still a freshman at Mercer University. For a while, Peyton Anderson was, to him, just the man in the front office—friendly and generous, it was said, but quite distant from a part-time reporter.

There was an election that November, and it meant a tremendous amount of work for the staffers of each paper. Even the part-timers were pressed into duty. Not only were there national and state races to cover, but elections had also been held in the surrounding counties and the city of Macon. When the winners had been declared and the last word was finally written that night, Peyton came to the newsroom.

"Okay, guys," he told the reporters and editors, "we've put out the paper. Come to my office."

The tired newspapermen trailed into Peyton's office and the publisher unlocked his liquor cabinet. He served them himself, circulating around the room, chatting with one, then another. He had a knack for relating to just about anyone. As the staff sat there discussing the election results and sipping the boss's liquor, young Reg Murphy decided that this was about as good as anything was ever going to get.

Murphy left Mercer soon after that and went to work for the *Telegraph* full time. He discovered that the Macon papers were absolutely fearless when it came to news coverage. If a reporter discovered corruption in state or local government, he was free to write about it. Although Peyton himself might have been under pressure from politicians and advertisers to suppress such stories, none of that pressure ever found its way to the reporters.

Peyton had strong feelings about drunk driving. The policy of both papers was, if there was a DUI arrest, it would be reported in the paper. One night a prominent local woman was arrested and charged with driving under the influence of alcohol. Reg duly wrote an account of it for the morning paper. Later that day, they learned the woman had taken an overdose of sleeping pills. She was found dead on her bed with the newspaper beside her. Murphy and the others were terribly shaken by this tragedy. Many people in the community demanded that the publication of these arrests stop, but Peyton would not hear of it.

"No," he said, "the way you keep a town from having so many deaths from drunk drivers killing other people is to publish the names." The policy continued unchanged.

Although the National Civil Rights Act was still some ten years in the future, protests against racial discrimination were already taking place all over the country. During the mid-fifties, the *Telegraph* and the *News* were much more moderate than most other southern papers in matters of race. Murphy and his fellow reporters were free to cover the early civil rights demonstrations and meetings of black groups when other newspapers were turning a blind eye to those events.

In 1955, the *Macon Telegraph and News* established its first Atlanta bureau and Reg Murphy was the reporter chosen to staff it. Bert Struby instructed him to cover the capitol for the two papers. There had been complaints that the Atlanta papers slanted political stories and Struby was determined the Macon papers would do nothing of the kind. "Just cover the straight story. That's all."

Peyton rarely interfered with his reporters, but Murphy had one standing order from him and that was to cover anything that had anything to do with the proposed interstate highway system around Macon. There were two possible routes under consideration for

Interstate 75. One would go through the city of Macon. The other would bypass it by fifteen or twenty miles to the west. Peyton firmly believed that Macon must not be bypassed. He knew that towns shunned by major highways were likely to dry up and die and he didn't plan to see that happen to Macon. Peyton didn't ask Murphy to slant the stories. He simply wanted to be kept constantly up to date on the project and pass that information along to his readers.

In an effort to influence the decision makers, Peyton joined with a number of civic and business leaders. The group was untiring in its lobbying of the politicians who would make the final choice. And that hard work paid off. When the route was finalized, the announcement was made that Interstates 75 and 16 would intersect in downtown Macon.

Reg Murphy was a talented reporter and, by the end of the decade, he had attracted the attention of some important people in Atlanta and the rest of the nation. Several suggested to him that he should apply for a Nieman Fellowship at Harvard University. The Nieman Fellowships were awarded to reporters, photographers, editors, and cartoonists for a year of independent study at Harvard to "promote and elevate journalism standards." Every applicant had to have permission from his employer before applying. If accepted, the applicant agreed to return to his employer after the fellowship ended and work there for a minimum of one full year.

With Peyton's approval, Murphy applied for and won a Nieman Fellowship. When it was over the following May, he returned to work with the *Telegraph and News*, and was once again put in charge of the Atlanta bureau. It was punishing work, trying to cover state politics for both a morning and afternoon paper, and Murphy was exhausted much of the time. At the end of 1960, he was offered the position of political editor for *The Atlanta Constitution*. It was an offer that might never come again and he took it, even though he had not fulfilled his agreement to return and work for the *Telegraph* for an entire year.

Peyton was furious at what he perceived as a betrayal. While they were civil when they met at various press functions over the years, the two men never again enjoyed a friendly relationship. Murphy went on to become editor of the *Atlanta Constitution*, publisher of both the *San Francisco Examiner* and the *Baltimore Sun*, and president of the National Geographic Society.

Peyton took a genuine interest in the people who worked for him. He knew the names of their spouses and their children. When one of them was in trouble, he did what he could to help. More than once, he stepped in and paid medical bills or loaned an employee enough money for the down payment to purchase a house. These generous gestures were made in private with no desire for recognition or repayment.

Peyton was always active in a number of organizations. In 1953, he was elected president of the Southern Newspaper Publishers Association and, the following year, chairman of the SNPA board. In 1956, President Eisenhower appointed him to the Board of Visitors at the United States Naval Academy, and in 1957 he was elected chairman of that board. He was reelected in 1958 and, in 1959, was appointed to the Academy's International Advisory Board.

While attending an SNPA meeting in 1954 in Point Clear, Alabama, Peyton received an important invitation. Before breakfast one morning, Eugene Yates, president of the Southern Company, came to his room. The two men sat on the verandah sipping coffee and Yates asked if Peyton would consider becoming a director of his company.

The publisher had some reservations about that. "It could put me in a position where there might be a conflict of interest. I hire editors and give them freedom to express themselves."

But Yates was insistent and Peyton finally agreed, with a caveat. "If there is ever a situation in which my editors don't have an understanding of what The Southern Company is doing, I'll have to resign."

Telegraph editor Bert Struby hired a new secretary in 1951. At eighteen, Barbara Fowler had no real business experience, but she was eager to do a good job and Struby wasn't concerned.

"I'll train you my own way," he declared.

Barbara settled happily into her new job. She liked her boss and soon became friendly with Peyton Anderson's secretary Jeannette Gausch. Barbara's office was right across the hall from the publisher's suite. She saw Peyton almost every day. He was pleasant and always had a cheerful word for her. In fact, everyone at the paper made her feel welcome.

Perhaps Barbara's favorite new acquaintance was Julia Northrop. Miss Julia still ran the library in the same no-nonsense fashion she had for nearly twenty years. She maintained that every-thing had a place, and she was the person who decided where that place was. No one at the paper wanted to take a chance of crossing her.

One morning Major Moore from the Stereotype Department intercepted Peyton just outside his office door. He was concerned about storage. In those days, mats the size of a full newspaper page were molded and made into plates to be used in the printing process. They were bulky items and Moore was looking for somewhere to store them when they were not in use. He thought the library was the perfect solution.

"Well, that's fine," Peyton said carefully. "Go talk to Aunt Julia about it."

"No," Moore said hesitantly, "no, *you* go tell her."

"*You* do it," Peyton insisted.

Barbara found the spectacle of two grown men afraid to talk to one elderly woman amusing. In the end, nobody talked to Miss Julia about the mats. Neither man was willing to risk upsetting her.

Barbara had never been afraid of Miss Julia, but the librarian was the most unconventional person she'd ever met. Although she was approaching retirement age, she didn't let the passing years slow her down. She made her own yogurt and even cut her own grass. She was plainspoken and convinced that women could accomplish anything they set their minds to. Barbara loved hearing her stories about living in a tent out west with her late husband. However, she drew the line at sharing the health drink Miss Julia called Vitamix. It was a home-made mixture of vegetables, pureed in a blender and Miss Julia declared it was what kept her healthy. Barbara tasted the dreadful concoction only once. That was enough to make her swear off it forever.

Peyton was a pleasure to work with. He rarely lost his temper and was easygoing about most things. He did, however, take exception to his employees going to Atlanta to shop in the big department stores there. "Y'all are traipsing off to Atlanta to spend your money there when people in Macon are advertising in our paper," he'd tell Jeannette and Barbara. "You need to spend your money here."

Only once did Barbara think Peyton might really lose his temper—with her as the object of his anger. She'd only been working at the paper a short time and Struby, Peyton, and the other managers were in a staff meeting. Jeannette had gone to lunch, leaving Barbara with strict instructions.

"They are not to be disturbed by anybody."

Barbara was determined to do a good job. When a middle-aged man bustled into the office and announced he wanted to see Peyton Anderson, she knew just what to do.

"I'm sorry, sir. He's in a staff meeting right now and can't be disturbed."

"But I need to see him. I'm Mills B. Lane, Jr."

He acted as if that should change things, but the name didn't mean a thing to Barbara. She held her ground and, after a few more minutes of futile insistence, Lane left. He was a bit upset, but Barbara was sure she'd done the right thing—until Jeannette came back.

"Don't you know who that *was?*" she asked, horrified.

When Barbara admitted she didn't, Jeannette explained that Lane was not only a good friend of Peyton Anderson's, but was chairman of the board of Citizens and Southern Bank—the newspapers' own bank.

Barbara was sure she'd be fired. When Peyton came out of his meeting and learned what happened, he was not pleased, but he didn't fire the young secretary. After explaining why he should always be available to Mills Lane, the incident he never mentioned again.

While working at the *Telegraph and News* Barbara Fowler met and fell in love with Carlton Hunnicutt who worked in the composing room. When she told Miss Julia that they planned to marry, the lady wasn't in favor of the idea. However, Carlton won her over in the end. They were married in 1957 and Barbara left the paper the next year. The couple kept in touch with Miss Julia until her death years later.

Loyalty was high on the list of virtues that Peyton Anderson admired and one he tried to practice. McKibbon Lane had served as chief counsel for the newspapers for many years. Every Tuesday morning he would leave his office and walk down the street to the Telegraph Building where he'd meet with Peyton and the other managers. Over coffee, they would discuss any legal matters that needed attention. When a new lawyer, Ed Sell, Jr., joined the small firm, Lane took him along to these meetings. McKibbon Lane died in 1956 and Sell discontinued the Tuesday coffee meetings. Lane had been the one taking part in those meetings and had only let him tag along. He would have felt he was being presumptuous going to the paper alone.

After Lane's death, there was a rush of attorneys trying to get the lucrative *Telegraph and News* business, but Ed Sell wasn't among them. He believed that he was too new in town to compete with the veteran lawyers trying to get the paper's business. But Peyton had liked the young attorney and felt a loyalty to Lane's firm. One morning he gave Sell a call and asked if he wanted to take over the representation of the papers. Sell accepted with pleasure, of course, and a long business and personal relationship began.

8

Corvettes, Crewcuts, and Politics

Kat Anderson was a gardener. She'd always loved growing things and was years ahead of her time in promoting earth-friendly techniques. She had strong ideas about composting and became furious when she saw someone burning leaves. Although she never did, her daughters were always afraid she'd stop the car and confront the offenders, directing them to compost their leaves and yard trimmings.

Over the years, she had transformed the yard on Oakcliff from scrub brush to a lush garden where azaleas, camellias, and other blooming shrubs and bulbs welcomed each spring with a riot of color. A creek at the back of the yard meandered through tall hardwood shade in an area that was left mostly natural. She always had several huge piles of compost in varying stages of decomposition. She called the rich, decaying matter "my chocolate pie" and joked with her family, saying, "When I die just roll me over in the compost."

With Katty away at Duke University and Deyerle wrapped up in the activities at Lanier Middle School, Kat was interested in finding something constructive to do with her time. She found it writing a weekly gardening column called "In Your Garden" for the *Telegraph* under the name Kate Greenleaf. The column began in 1951 and ran until she retired in 1965.

Deyerle Anderson turned sixteen in 1953 and got her driver's license soon afterwards. Peyton approached the occasion the same way he would a contract negotiation with one of the unions, presenting her with the following:

TO: Miss Deyerle Anderson:

Since you are now 16 years of age and have procured your driver's license, you shall be privileged to use Little Kat's 1951 Ford Sedan while she is away or, with consent, either of the other cars at the house.

I congratulate you on your ability, and am particularly proud over your patience in becoming eligible for a license. You have been taught how to drive properly, so continue to do so and drive with caution.

The following rules apply to your use of a car:

Car is for your use and pleasure. You are NOT to permit any one else to drive it, nor are you to drive any one else's car.

You are to operate car with courtesy to all and in accordance with all laws and traffic regulations. Should you get arrested, you are to appear in court and pay out of your allowance any fine.

Any accidents or collisions with people or property are to be reported to me and to Jesse Davis immediately, with all details.

Car is not to be used in any parade or decorated in any manner. Windows or windshields are to be free from any stickers that will in any way impair full vision.

You are to be home and car in garage at 6:30 P.M., or by dark, which ever comes first. No deviations are to be made without my consent.

In case you violate any rule, car is not to be used until proper approval by me. Keys will be turned over to me.

Television was just making its appearance in American homes. In September 1953, Macon's first television station, WMAZ, took to the airways. Peyton Anderson, who could always be counted on to have the newest and most unusual gadgets, was one of the first people in Macon to own a television set. In the evenings, the lights in the houses dimmed as families gathered around the new invention.

Dragnet and *I Love Lucy* were suddenly part of the national consciousness.

Katty Anderson married John Bleibtreu on 26 February 1954. It was a small evening wedding celebrated in the Andersons' home. Deyerle was Katty's only attendant and John's father was his best man. The Reverend Stewart Matthews, rector of St. Paul's Episcopal Church, performed the service. At the end of the ceremony, Rabbi Newton Friedman of Temple Beth Israel offered a blessing. After the honeymoon, Katty and John went to live in New York City.

A few weeks later, Peyton surprised his friends and family by purchasing a new car—and what a car it was. He'd heard about a new Chevrolet model called the Corvette and seen pictures of it as well. That, he decided, was the car he wanted. He went to see Bob Dunlap at Dunlap Chevrolet and announced his intention, but he was disappointed. Bob didn't have a Corvette on the lot. Neither did any other nearby dealer. But Peyton had made up his mind and nothing else would satisfy him. Bob made a lot of telephone calls and was finally successful. His friend Hobby Law, who owned Newton Chevrolet in Chattanooga, Tennessee, had one Corvette on his lot. Peyton declared he would take it sight unseen.

The next day he and Deyerle flew up to Chattanooga where Peyton took possession of the brand new Corvette. Gleaming white with a bright red interior, it was the most gorgeous car Deyerle had ever seen. They drove it back to Macon that same day, turning heads all along the way. Once in North Georgia, a state patrolman pulled them over, but he wasn't interested in giving Peyton a ticket.

"What kind of car is *this*?" he asked when he approached them. Peyton was delighted with his interest and spent some time showing off the car's bells and whistles.

Driving around Macon in Georgia's first Corvette was great fun. Peyton relished the attention it brought him. He especially enjoyed Sunday mornings when he could drive up to the front of the church and pick up Kat as she came out. After a couple of years, though, the excitement wore off.

Rather than sell it, Peyton made the Corvette a company car and assigned it to state news editor George Landry. George had a fine time driving the sports car all over Middle Georgia. Once he was headed to an outlying county to cover a news story and was impatient to get there. As he sped along a back road, he came upon several cars driving very slowly. Poking along that way wasn't going to get him where he wanted to go soon enough. He waited until the way ahead was clear, then gunned the powerful engine, swung into the other lane and passed car after car. It wasn't until he'd passed the eighth or ninth car that he saw the hearse leading the procession. He was so embarrassed that he sped away as quickly as he could.

Unfortunately, a Corvette with words the *Macon Telegraph* on its sides, was a hard vehicle to miss. By the time George returned to the office, Peyton had already fielded several angry phone calls from people complaining that George had been disrespectful in passing a funeral procession. George managed to explain the situation to Peyton's satisfaction and continued driving the Corvette until the engine eventually blew up.

Two years after Katty's wedding, there was a second ceremony at the Anderson home. Eighteen-year-old Deyerle married Russell Hanson. In an echo of their own parents' feelings of twenty years before, Kat and Peyton thought their youngest daughter was not old enough to marry. But Deyerle was a determined young woman. When they saw that they couldn't dissuade her, they gave in and celebrated with her.

The noon wedding took place on 24 August 1956, and was attended by only the immediate family. This time Katty was Deyerle's only attendant. After the ceremony, a bridal luncheon was served. Champagne was poured, the bride and groom were toasted, the guests drank their champagne, and, one by one in keeping with a family tradition, the glasses were thrown and smashed in the big front-room fireplace.

Shortly after Deyerle's wedding Peyton got his first crewcut. He'd neatly parted and combed his silver hair to the side for so long that his changed appearance startled the people who knew him, but it soon became his signature look. When asked why he'd made the change, Peyton just laughed and said he did something crazy when each of his daughters got married. Katty's marriage had brought on the purchase of the Corvette. Deyerle's made him cut his hair.

When the Georgia Power Company dammed the Oconee River in 1953, the result was increased electrical production for Middle Georgia and a 15,000-acre lake. Lake Sinclair became the focus of Middle Georgia water recreation, and in early 1955, Kat and Peyton Anderson began construction of one of the first lakeshore houses. It was a large, two-story cedar home located on a point of land and they called it Peyton's Place.

A guest book kept by the family indicated that temporary completion of the house was accomplished at 4:00 P.M. on 3 July 1955. "Pre-completion guests had to wash dishes, install slipcovers, hang draperies, lay carpets and work like the devil—and they did." Those pre-completion guests during that Fourth of July holiday were Lucile and Red Roberts, Ruth, Coley and Nancy Moughon, Russell Hanson and Margaret and Joan Sancken.

Peyton filled the lake house with the kinds of amenities he wanted and, more importantly, with those things he believed would please his guests. There was a big kitchen with a huge pantry that he kept fully stocked, perhaps even overstocked. He was never content to have one of anything. There were three jars of mayonnaise and two bottles of ketchup and four bags of sugar. Window air-conditioning units had been installed throughout the house, but Peyton didn't like using them, insisting that they made the whole place vibrate. The entire house was wired with speakers, and guests always knew when Peyton was up for the day. Music would blare throughout the house—sometimes Percy Faith, sometimes Frank Sinatra, sometimes military marches. The theme from *Bridge on the River Kwai* was one of his favorites. Peyton believed that, when he was awake, everyone else should be, too.

He loved the water and water skiing. There were stories that he'd enjoyed the sport so much he'd even managed to do a bit of it in the Pacific during World War II. At Lake Sinclair, Peyton had two boats—a pontoon boat, which he called the playpen, for lazy trips around the lake, and a ski boat. He would pull people on skis all day long and particularly liked teaching first-timers to ski. Children were his favorite students. When his niece Denny O'Callaghan and her friends would come for an afternoon of fun, he'd be determined that every one of them would know how to ski by the time they left.

"If you don't get up this time," he shout back to a water-treading, potential skier, "we're going to run over you!" He was teasing, of course, but the little girls' eyes did get a bit bigger and they tried a little harder to get up on the skis.

Peyton usually preferred driving the boat to skiing, but he could be talked into taking a more physical role. That most often happened when he knew he'd have a good-sized audience. Then he'd allow himself to be pulled behind the boat and, as it sped past the house, he'd grin and wave to the people on the dock.

Kat wasn't especially fond of the water, but she was happy to sit on the porch and read a book, while her family and guests enjoyed the lake.

For Christmas of 1957, Peyton's friends and employees at the paper got together and gave him a small, motorized watercraft. More than anything else, it looked like a motorcycle, with a seat and handles for steering, and was a precursor to today's jet ski. It was bright red and Peyton loved it. He christened it Sputnik, after the Russian satellite that had orbited the earth a few months before. Someone in nearby Milledgeville quipped, "Peyton Anderson's got everything on Sinclair but a submarine." If he'd been able to do it, he probably would have had a submarine as well.

The Andersons put two house trailers on their Lake Sinclair lot and made them available for any *Telegraph and News* employees who wanted to use them. Carlton and Barbara Hunnicutt and Harold and Nita Wood were some of the employees that took advantage of that offer. If Peyton were at the house when there were visitors in the trailers, he'd sometimes stop in and visit with them, maybe taking some steaks from his freezer for them to grill.

David and Blanche Redding and their son David, Jr., were frequent guests at the lake house. Peyton taught young David to ski and allowed him to use Sputnik. Visits to Peyton's Place became high points in the young man's life. David's association with Peyton wasn't limited to the time at Lake Sinclair. The boy was active in Scouting, and when he was going for his Eagle badge, Peyton was one of the people who wrote a recommendation for him.

The Lake Sinclair house was not limited to the entertainment of friends and family. Peyton often invited business associates to join him there. Among those he entertained at Lake Sinclair were Congressman Carl Vinson and Dr. Alex Huhn of Zurich, manager of the Swiss Newspaper Publishers Association.

The country experienced an economic boom in the years after World War II. The newspapers prospered along with the rest of Macon and, in the late fifties, Peyton was in a position to pay off the mortgage on the paper. He chartered a plane and he, Treasurer Ernest Hardin, and Chief Counsel Ed Sell flew to North Carolina. When they arrived at the Jefferson Standard Building, they entered an elevator in the lobby for transport to the fourth floor. As the doors closed, they were surprised to hear a pleasant, female voice.

"Lobby ... going up. Passing the second level ... passing the third level ... arriving level four."

While the others laughed about a talking elevator, Ernest Hardin was unnerved by the verbal machinery. He couldn't get off the car fast enough. When their transaction was over and the newspapers belonged to Peyton, free and clear, the four Georgians left the office. Ernest allowed himself to be guided into the elevator, but gave a relieved sigh when he stepped out into the lobby.

The first Joint Civilian Orientation Conference was hosted by the Department of Defense in 1948. The weeklong program was designed to acquaint public opinion leaders with the country's state of national defense. In March 1957, Secretary of Defense C. E. Wilson invited Peyton to participate in the Joint Civilian Orientation Conference in May.

Peyton accepted and was present on May 2 for the opening conference reception at the Mayflower Hotel in Washington, DC. The next morning the group met at the Pentagon for discussions by high-level military and civilian leaders of the Department of Defense. The rest of their time was spent in the field. They toured Quantico for a demonstration of Marine combat tactics. They were transported by military aircraft to the US Naval Station at Jacksonville, Florida, to observe naval sea and air exercises, then to Eglin AFB in Florida. The conference ended with a visit to Ft. Benning, Georgia.

That same year Kat and Peyton became grandparents for the first time. Joshua Bleibtreu was born in April, followed by Reid Hanson in May. Adam Bleibtreu entered the world in December 1958 and Laura Hanson was born two months later.

Perhaps prompted by his new status as grandparent, Peyton purchased another flashy car—a 1957 red and white Ford Thunderbird. Once again he turned heads driving around town. The new car also provided him with a reason to acquire another gadget. When he learned that there was an instrument that would mount on the dash of his car, judge the speed and consider the destination, and provide an estimated time of arrival, he had to have it.

Mills B. Lane, Jr., decided in 1958 that he wanted to purchase the two Savannah, Georgia, newspapers, the *Morning News* and the *Evening Press*. Alvah Chapman would be his partner in the enterprise and he asked Peyton to help him negotiate the deal. Lane and Peyton had been friends for years and Peyton was well acquainted with fellow SNPA member Chapman, so he was happy to do what he could. He performed well, bringing the two sides together and brokering the sale. Lane and Chapman were the new owners of the Savannah papers and Chapman became the publisher and president of the resulting corporation.

Peyton had met Lyndon Johnson several times and always found him to be a charming, intelligent man. The two kept in touch over the years, usually by letter, sharing opinions, offers of help and asking for the occasional favor. One of those requests for a favor came in March 1960. Peyton wrote to Johnson and asked if he would meet with the editors of the two Macon newspapers, Bill Ott and Joe Parham, on an upcoming trip to Washington. Johnson immediately arranged a meeting and gave the editors as much time as they needed when they visited the capital.

When, the following October, Johnson was running as John Kennedy's vice presidential candidate and campaigned in seven Southern states, Peyton was able to return the favor. He hosted the senator's visit to Macon. He, along with Senator Herman Talmadge, Governor Ernest Vandiver, and Congressman Carl Vinson, met Johnson when he landed at Cochran Field. After the candidate made some brief remarks at the airport, the group drove to Mercer University for Law Day where Johnson spoke to a crowd of about 3,000 people.

Back in Washington, Johnson wrote to Peyton, thanking him for his hospitality: "One of the pleasant memories of this national campaign, which is now so near its close, is my visit to your area." He then asked a favor. His wife Ladybird was assembling a collection of newspaper stories, editorials and cartoons about his candidacy. Johnson asked if Peyton could send him the stories about his visit to Macon from the *Telegraph* and the *News*.

The day before the national election, Peyton answered Johnson's letter. He had sent the requested material in a separate mailing. After wishing the candidate good luck in the vote, he closed with: "Hope the rigors of the campaign were not too telling and that you will be in there pitching for the new organizational set up."

The next day the Kennedy-Johnson ticket was victorious and Peyton's friend was now vice president of the United States.

Although he declared he wasn't fond of leaving the country, Peyton and Kat did some international traveling in the sixties. They toured several Asian countries in 1961 and Peyton sent the folks at the office a postcard from Hong Kong that read:

"Wonderful time—every place gets better, so looking forward to Bangkok tonight. Transportation from jet to rickshaw to sampan to strolling down Nathan Road. Bought more unneeded clothes such as red silk—and I do mean red—dinner coat—though not happy about it. Kat has her white brocaded Chinese dress. This is without a doubt greatest place for salesmanship I've ever seen. P."

A few years later they visited Europe, and there were also a number of trips to the Caribbean, arguably Peyton's favorite place on earth. Hunting and fishing were activities he particularly enjoyed. Kat went with him on many of those outings, and when she didn't go, he'd take friends and employees. His generous nature often led to his buying guests fishing outfits or tackle once they reached their destination.

Business demanded travel as well. He and Kat regularly attended the New York American Newspaper Publishers Association conferences. New Orleans was a favorite location for the Southern Newspaper Publishers Association's annual meeting and Peyton always made sure Ed Sell came along because he knew how much his friend enjoyed the Louisiana city. They usually stayed at the Roosevelt Hotel and were good customers of some of the city's finest restaurants—Commander's Palace, Brennan's, and Galatoire's.

When they were home, the Andersons entertained frequently and the barbecue grill in the side yard was kept busy. Sometimes Peyton served up the yield of his latest fishing or hunting trip. He and Kat also spent a great deal of time at the lake house and there was always great excitement deciding who would be invited for the weekends. Deyerle and her family were frequent guests, as were the Reddings. Ed and Pree Sell also visited from time to time. Once in a while Ed's law partner John Comer and his wife Mary would make the drive out to the lake house with them.

9

Friendship

The make up of the Macon newspapers was changing. In 1957, Bert Struby was elevated to general manager of the *Telegraph and News* and, a year later, was made executive vice president. At the same time, William A. Ott, who'd joined the *Telegraph* staff in 1950, was named editor.

It wasn't only the staff that was experiencing change. For some time it had been obvious that the *Telegraph and News* was outgrowing its Cherry Street home. The company already owned land between Broadway and Fifth Street on Riverside Drive, and in 1958 they purchased some adjacent acreage near the river from the Macon, Dublin, and Savannah Railroad. That acquisition gave them enough space for a new building.

Architects Francis K. Hall and J. Edmond Ferguson designed it and construction began in January 1960. Peyton had a standing order concerning materials: if it could be found in Macon, it would be bought in Macon. One year later, the building was finished and ready for occupancy. It was supremely functional as well as stylish. The public entrance was through large glass doors into a three-story lobby, the centerpiece of which was a freestanding circular staircase of concrete and terrazzo that led to the third floor. Dumbwaiters and pneumatic tubes provided quick communication between departments. Fixed vertical aluminum louvers were set at a sixty-six-degree angle to the building to deflect the sun's heat and glare. A fifty-foot parking plaza and a flat roof, reinforced for helicopter landing and take off, completed the design.

Before the heavy machinery and employees moved in, the huge cast-pewter eagle that had graced the Cherry Street building was moved to the new building on Broadway. The operation required a crew of men, a big flatbed truck and a crane. Once the eagle, recently regilded, was affixed to a ledge over the front entrance, the building was ready. On February 18, the move was complete and the papers had relocated to the new building without missing an issue. The cost of construction and the move was $1.25 million.

The employees presented a plaque to Peyton at a reception in the lobby of the new building on 7 April 1961. It read:

Presented To
PEYTON ANDERSON
on the occasion of the
opening of the new plant and office of
The Macon Telegraph
and
The Macon News
in the year Nineteen Hundred and Sixty One
HIS WISDOM AND COURAGE
HIS UNDERSTANDING AND LOYALTY
HIS UNBLEMISHED INTEGRITY
AND HIS LOVE FOR PEOPLE
HAVE INSPIRED ALL
WHO WORK WITH HIM.
The Employees

Eugene Anderson did not live to see the move into the new building. He was ninety-four years old when he died on 1 March 1961. This remarkable man had been writing "Around the Circle" for the *Macon Telegraph* since 1946. Although he'd been ill for several weeks, he'd continued writing his column, with his wife's help, from his hospital bed in Forsyth. His last column was sent in the day before his death and appeared on the editorial page the same day his obituary was run. He was buried in Riverside Cemetery in Macon.

The same year the new building opened, Peyton was elected to the board of directors of Citizens and Southern Bank in Atlanta. In the press release, Chairman of the Board Mills Lane was quoted as saying "Peyton Anderson's wide newspaper experience and vast knowledge of Georgia will make him a most valuable asset to the C&S Board."

Peyton left the editorials to his editors, the people he'd hired to do the jobs. "I give the editors free rein," he often said. "I serve as a sounding board to them. I'll play the devil's advocate and, if they can convince me of their argument, they can put it in the paper."

The push for integration had begun in earnest in 1961. Freedom Riders were on the roads in Alabama and Mississippi. In Georgia, the first black students attended classes at the University of Georgia. Like most southern towns in the sixties, Macon experienced its share of racial tension. The *Telegraph and News* took a moderating view, trying to keep the community calm.

In February 1962, black leaders in Macon announced a boycott of the privately owned Bibb Transit Company buses "until we can ride in dignity and without risk of arrest". They were demanding freedom of choice in seating and the hiring of blacks as drivers and mechanics.

On the same day that U-2 pilot Francis Gary Powers returned to the United States, 3,000 black citizens rallied at the Allen Chapel on Pursley Street in Macon and called for a boycott. The story of the rally was carried on the front page of the *Telegraph* the Monday morning that the boycott began.

Charges and accusations flew between the bus company and the protesters. Young blacks pelted buses with stones and bricks and some passengers were injured. On Saturday night, February 17, a group of white men drove up to a black dance hall on Broadway and fired a shotgun into the crowd. Two of the club's patrons were wounded. It was a frightening time and for a while neither Macon's black or white citizens felt safe.

The morning after the shooting, the lead editorial in the *Telegraph* carried the heading "Macon Leaders Must Act to End Community Strife". It read in part:

"Macon has a vast reservoir of calm, intelligent, courageous citizens who realize the community will suffer great harm by a prolonged continuation of the bus dispute. It is time for this leadership to make itself felt by positive action.

"Each day that passes without a solution being found gives more encouragement for lawless elements of both races to do their dirty work."

The editorial commended the mayor for meeting with both sides and chastised the sheriff for failing to take part in the meeting.

"Macon has the good sense to solve its problems without staining its reputation with hatred, bitterness and violence," it concluded. "Let the coming week be one of constructive thinking and action to mend the damage done during the past week." And the community responded accordingly. The bus boycott was concluded without further violence.

The Anderson family was changing with the times. The early sixties brought Peyton and Kat two more grandchildren—Jason Bleibtreu in 1961 and Peyton Hanson in 1963. Being a part of their grandchildren's lives was important to them. It wasn't difficult to do with Deyerle's children because they lived in and around Macon. But Katty and her family were out of state. The grandparents had to make the most of their occasional visits and kept in touch with frequent letters and phone calls. Peyton especially enjoyed corresponding with his grandchildren, even when they were quite young, and saved every letter he ever received from them.

When Kat and Peyton returned from their Asian tour in 1961, an awkwardly printed note was waiting for them. Five-year-old Joshua Bleibtreu had written: "Welcome back. I've missed you."

About a year later, Joshua wrote again, this time with the assistance of his father John, who wrote:

> Looks as though Joshy is going to be your best Yankee correspondent. He loves to write to you. I thought then, perhaps that if he dictated his letters to me on the typewriter, I could exercise a measure of editorial control. But he can read—not well, but enough to know when I'm changing things around. So he keeps me honest.
>
> Adam likes to write to you, too, but he seems to consider you Santa Claus and his letters consist of a series of 'gimmes.' I won't mail this latest one. But Joshy's will be mailed.

Joshua's unedited letter to his grandfather revealed an interest in his Aunt Deyerle's horse: "When you go out to see the horse, please tell me all the things you need to look after a horse. I know about blankets and we have some nice warm blankets—but I don't know about the things you need to make their shoes bigger or littler.

"This time maybe I'll come over to see you. But not now. I'm not eight years old now. And it'll have to be in the afternoon because I go to school in the morning."

In 1956 Georgian Paul Anderson, who had no connection with Peyton's family, won the Olympic gold metal for weightlifting in the super-heavyweight division. No American ever matched that feat again. Paul was from Toccoa, up in the north Georgia mountains, where he and his wife Glenda were very active in their church. The young couple had a dream of someday opening a youth home where abandoned or troubled children could be loved and cared for.

The Piggly Wiggly supermarket chain hired Anderson to promote new store openings. As part of the celebration, he would put on a weight-lifting demonstration. His appearance always guaranteed the store a big audience. When a grand opening was planned for Vidalia in 1961, Paul and Glenda drove down to the small town in Middle Georgia where Paul amazed the crowd with his strength. Afterwards, he and Glenda spent some time talking with a few local people, including the sheriff. The townspeople told the Andersons that they were hoping to start a boys' home. Paul and Glenda confided their own dream. That was the beginning.

Their organization was incorporated in January 1962 and Paul and Glenda took in their first children while still living at a local motel. Eventually they moved into a big white house on a rural tract of land. They built their first cottage there in 1964 and hired a single man as a houseparent to live with several boys.

Meanwhile, Paul continued making public appearances all over the southeast, but he was no longer promoting grocery stores. Now he was raising money for the Paul Anderson Youth Home. When he spoke to a civic club in Macon and demonstrated his might by lifting a table with five men sitting on it, Peyton Anderson was in the audience. While Paul's strength was extraordinary, Peyton was much more impressed by his dedication to teaching character and patriotism to children. He stayed after the meeting to talk with the strong man. That was the beginning of a bond between the two men that would last until Peyton's death and beyond.

Peyton made numerous contributions to the Paul Anderson Home. He stayed in touch with them over the years and occasionally visited there himself. One of his gifts enabled them to build a new cottage that was named in his honor.

The consistent quality of his newspapers and Peyton's work with the ANPA brought Peyton a certain amount of national prominence. No one was surprised when he was one of a number of Georgia editors and publishers invited to a White House luncheon with President John Kennedy.

On 6 February 1963, Peyton flew to Washington and checked into the Mayflower Hotel. At 12:30 the next afternoon, he climbed into a taxi with three other men: Jack Williams, Jr., of Waycross, Quimby Melton of Griffin, and his long-time friend Max Nussbaum from Moultrie. A ten-minute ride took the four newspapermen to the Northeast Gate of the White House. Inside the door, they were led to a large silver bowl where each drew a slip of paper to determine where they would be seated at the luncheon. Williams was delighted to learn he would be to the President's immediate left. Peyton's draw placed him just across the table.

After a reception in the Blue Room where President Kennedy managed to shake the hand of everyone present and exchange at least a few words, the group moved to the State Dining Room. There, for two and half hours, they worked their way through the issues of the day while enjoying rack of lamb, Potatoes Paille and baked Alaska.

Congressman Carl Vinson had been a friend and associate of the Andersons for many years. He began representing the state of Georgia in the House of Representatives in 1914, when Peyton was only five years old. On 16 November 1963, he celebrated his eightieth birthday. Although Peyton was unable to attend the celebration, he wrote his old friend a warm, congratulatory letter. When Vinson wrote back, the congressman couldn't help but mention the dreadful events that had just occurred in Dallas and shaken the entire country.

> "The terrible tragedy that befell the nation last Friday will not cause me to change my plan to retire at the end of my present term—January 3, 1965.
>
> "You have certainly been a true friend and I want you to know that I shall remember and cherish your friendship to my last day.
>
> "With kindest regards and best wishes I remain
> Sincerely, your friend,
> Carl Vinson"

Four months after he became president, Lyndon Johnson wrote to Peyton:

"Our mutual friend Dick Russell brought me your greetings and best wishes and I wish to assure you of my appreciation.

"I remember very pleasantly our association several years ago. I hope we will have an opportunity to renew our acquaintance.

Sincerely,

Lyndon"

Peyton answered with reminiscences of his own, demonstrating the warmth he felt for the man: "I recall your visit to Warner Robins with Carl Vinson on his first plane trip, and your visit to Macon for Mercer University Law Day with great pleasure. You are a great guy!

"You describe your job as President correctly as awesome, but I know of no one, through personality, dedication or experience, more able to handle it. You belong in the White House and Georgia will do its part to keep you there."

Peyton was as good as his word. He did everything he could to get LBJ elected in 1964. In May, he attended Governor Carl Sanders' legislative breakfast honoring Lyndon Johnson. And when the President campaigned in Georgia in the fall of that year, Peyton was there to welcome him to Macon.

After a motorcade down Cherry Street, Johnson made a speech in front of City Hall. Peyton, Governor Sanders, and other dignitaries stood beside him. In that speech, he referred to Peyton as "my very good friend." Laura Nelle was in the crowd of several thousand people and beamed with pride at that description.

"Does Peyton really know the President?" a friend asked her.

Laura Nelle smiled. "I believe he does."

Although most of those assembled on Poplar Street were Johnson supporters, there were a fair number of dissenters in the crowd. This was the Vietnam era and the anti-war sentiment was gaining strength across the country.

The next day, Peyton wrote to the President:

I am most grateful for the kind remarks you made about me yesterday. When you win the election next Tuesday, you will be an even better president. If I can assist you in any way in those duties, let me know.

Our friendship has been consistent and I hope it can bring about a more frequent contact between us. I'm available, Mr. President.

The rudeness of some of the crowd yesterday was very embarrassing to me, but as usual, you were gracious. My apologies for them, they knew not what they were doing.

Macon has for some 25 years been a part of your constituency. Your desire to continue to support our growth is most appreciated and we look forward to being of service to our great country and our greatest President.

Lyndon Johnson won the election by a landslide, but much to Peyton Anderson's embarrassment, Bibb County was solidly in the Barry Goldwater column when the votes were counted.

Friendship was important to Anderson. He and David Redding had been friends for many years. For much of that time, David had worked for the Joseph E. Neel Company, but he was anxious to go into business on his own. When he was ready to take the chance, Peyton was right there with him. He was instrumental in lining up much of the financing for the project and even put up half of the money himself. Redding purchased Macon Tent and Awning in 1964. Peyton served on the board of the new company and, a few years later when the business was established and doing well, he sold his interest in it to his old friend for the exact amount he'd originally invested.

Kat continued writing her gardening column through the early sixties, but she began experiencing health problems and retired in

1965. Although she no longer wrote about it, she never grew tired of gardening. Even when she wasn't physically able to get out and do it herself, she had yardmen that carried out her specific orders. She could name every plant in the yard and explain just what sort of care it needed.

Changes continued to come and many long-held habits and beliefs were being discarded by the younger generation. Macon and its citizens weren't immune. Deyerle Hanson had begun reconsidering the direction her life was taking. She'd read Betty Friedan and decided she should go to work. She had confidence in her writing ability. After all, she'd been taught by the best—her father had always declared he could teach anybody to write. Still she wasn't sure how he'd take her decision to join the work force.

She waited until Peyton was out of town, then went down to the newspaper, met with Joe Parham and asked to be hired in the newsroom as a reporter. Joe was diplomatic in his answer. He gave her a guardedly favorable response and said she could expect a final answer in a few days. Then, when Peyton returned to town, Joe asked him if it was all right to hire his daughter.

Peyton gave his approval and Deyerle went to work for Jay Trawick, who was then the managing editor. Trawick took the young woman under his wing, teaching her how to write for a newspaper. She caught on quickly. Deyerle worked for the *Telegraph* for several years, starting off with feature stories and eventually becoming the women's editor and the food editor.

On 5 June 1966 Peyton was awarded the Algernon Sydney Sullivan medallion at the Mercer University commencement exercises. The medallions were sponsored by the New York Southern Society and presented annually to a prominent leader for distinguished public service, and to outstanding students in the year's graduating class.

Over the years, Peyton had owned a number of watercraft and a variety of cars, but there was another mode of transportation that interested him as well. He became fascinated with the possibilities that helicopters might bring to the news business. Some people chalked it up to his well-known love of toys and gadgets, but others saw his interest as visionary.

Peyton purchased two Bell Helicopters and hired a Macon native as his pilot. R. L. Leggett had recently retired from the Army after twenty-seven years' service. A Vietnam veteran, his last assignment had been Aviation Battalion Commander and Division Aviation Staff Officer for the Third Armored Division in Europe.

Newscopters, Inc. was formed in November 1967, with Peyton as chairman of the board, Leggett as president, Bert Struby as vice president, Ed Sell as secretary, and Jeannette Gausch as treasurer.

"The growth potential for this company is based on the extension of news coverage, the expeditious processing of news, transporting bulk loads of newspapers to distribution points, support of promotions, public service, and leasing time to Middle Georgia enterprises," Peyton was quoted in a *Macon News* article.

The helicopters were based at Lewis Wilson Airport and six afternoons a week one would fly to downtown Macon, land on top of the Telegraph and News Building and pick up bundles of the *Macon News*. Fifteen minutes later, the aircraft put down at Westgate Shopping Center where carriers waited to deliver the papers in the Westgate, Bloomfield, and South Macon areas. The news department also had access to the helicopters for covering events all over Middle Georgia.

Peyton enjoyed the aircraft as much as anyone. He had a landing pad built in the yard of his Oakcliff Road house and it wasn't unusual for him to climb aboard one of the helicopters and fly to Lake Sinclair, where they'd whirl over the lake or land at the country club.

When boarding one of the copters, Peyton would sometimes jokingly quiz the pilot.

"Do you love your wife?"

"Of course, I do," Leggett would answer.

"Okay, I'll fly with you. Just wanted to make sure you want to get home again."

The following year, Peyton had a perfect opportunity to show off not only his newspapers, but the helicopters, too. Several newspaper executives flew into Macon for a meeting at the *Telegraph*. Peyton was there when they got off the plane at the Macon airport and a *Telegraph* photographer snapped a picture him greeting them. Then the photographer dashed to a waiting helicopter and flew the negative back to the paper where a plate was made of it. Moments later, it was put on the press.

The visitors were driven from the airport to the Telegraph and News Building. Once in the front door, they were led to the pressroom. There, on the front page of the *Macon News*, literally hot off the presses, was the photograph of their arrival in Macon.

Unfortunately, Newscopters, Inc. was not as profitable as Peyton had hoped. The business never really got established in Middle Georgia and was sold in 1969.

10

A Protégé for Life

Young people were important to Peyton Anderson. He enjoyed talking to them, hearing their views of the world and doing what he could to point them in the right direction. One of these was Wyatt Thomas Johnson.

Tommy Johnson was a student at Lanier High School for Boys in Macon when he first became involved with the local newspapers. Every year, the English teachers at his school were asked to submit students' names for the position of sports stringers at the *Telegraph and News*. It was a part-time job and paid accordingly, but when the teacher suggested it to Johnson, he was interested.

He went down to the paper and met with sports editor Sam Glassman, who explained that the duties of the position were attending local sporting events—basketball, baseball and football games—and bringing the scores in to the paper so that they could be included in the next morning's edition. The job sounded just fine to young Johnson and he was hired. He began working for the *Telegraph* in 1954, when he was in the ninth grade.

Under Glassman's gruff tutelage, the young boy learned how to keep scores at these events and how to write short accounts of them. Glassman taught him hunt-and-peck typing and the fundamentals of being a reporter. Johnson fell in love with the work and with the people at the paper. He was so inspired by what he was learning that he became the editor of his high school newspaper during his senior year.

As graduation approached, Bill Ott, then the managing editor, and Jim Chapman, the city editor, talked with Glassman about the boy's future. Finally they brought him in and asked what he planned to do after he graduated.

"Well," the boy said uncertainly, "I'd really like to go to college and study journalism, but I haven't made any plans yet."

He didn't tell them that he had no money for school, but they probably realized it. Tommy's family had been going through some hard times. His father was disabled and his mother worked at a grocery store on Columbus Road.

Bill Ott went to talk to Peyton about the boy, and the next afternoon, Tommy Johnson was brought to the publisher's office. He was nervous, of course, and ill at ease. Although he'd seen the publisher a few times during his years with the paper, he'd never actually met him. Peyton shook his hand and told him to sit down.

"You've done a good job for the paper," he said. "Bill Ott and Jim Chapman and Sam Glassman have all told me how hard you work."

Johnson didn't know what to say. He just nodded his head.

Then Peyton got to the point of the meeting. The paper would pay for his education at the University of Georgia on the condition that he commuted back to Macon every weekend to continue working for them. Johnson accepted the offer with gratitude and the promise that Mr. Anderson would not be sorry. He started his freshman year at Georgia that fall.

Throughout the school year, he left campus every Friday afternoon and made the two-hour drive back to Macon. He arrived there just in time to go to work. Friday nights were big nights for high school sports and Johnson rushed from one game to the next, making notes and keeping score.

During his freshman year, his friend and mentor, Sam Glassman died. Suddenly, Johnson found himself the senior weekend staffer in the sports department. Not only was he busy covering the events, he was doing more and more work on the desk. After a while, a new sports editor, Harley Bowers was hired. Johnson worked well for Bowers and came to admire him tremendously.

Although his schedule was a punishing one, Johnson's association with the newspaper didn't keep him from leading a full college life. He joined a fraternity, became the editor of the university newspaper and was a battalion commander in the ROTC. But he didn't party with the other guys on the weekends. Every Friday he climbed in the car and drove back to Macon. Part of the reason he did, of course, was that he had an obligation, but it was more than that. He was in love with the whole profession. The people he worked with at the newspaper encouraged and taught him. They taught him so well, in fact, that there were times in the classrooms at Georgia that he felt he knew more about a subject than what was being taught.

When a serious injury prevented him from entering the Army after his 1963 graduation, Johnson went home to Macon. As he had for the last several summers, he went back to work for the *Telegraph*. Shortly after his return, Peyton Anderson called him to his office for a meeting.

"Tommy, what is it you most want to do with your life?"

The answer came without any thought. "I want to be a publisher, just like you."

Peyton was pleased with the answer and Johnson was eager to share some exciting news with him.

"Mr. Anderson, I've been offered a graduate scholarship at the University of North Carolina to get my master's degree in journalism."

He expected Peyton to be as happy as he was, so the publisher's next words were a surprise. "If you intend to be a publisher one day, you don't need any more journalism. You've had journalism at Georgia. You've had journalism all the way through here at the paper. You need to learn business."

Then he made Johnson a most astonishing offer. "If you can be accepted to the Harvard Business School, I'll pay your way."

Peyton had always wanted to attend the Harvard Business School himself, but never had the opportunity. Now there was a chance he could give someone else that experience. Of course, it wasn't a very realistic idea. It was already June. Applying this late to graduate school, especially one so prestigious, was unheard of. But that didn't stop them from trying.

Bill Ott wrote letters to the Admissions Department and to the Dean of Harvard Business School, explaining that Tom had intended to go into the military, but had been injured at Fort Benning and was unable to follow that career. They were surprised and pleased when word came back from Massachusetts that Johnson could send in his application. Soon afterwards, they learned he'd been accepted.

Tommy continued working through the summer, preparing to leave for Harvard in the fall. But there was more than education going on in the young man's life that year. Just before he left for Massachusetts, he went to Peyton with great news. He'd fallen in love with a wonderful woman, Edwina Chastain of Athens, and they planned to marry.

Peyton's reaction was like a splash of cold water. He told Tom that marriage was a terrible mistake right then. It had nothing to do with Edwina, he just believed that the young man should be fully concentrating on his education. A wife, and the ultimate possibility of a family, would be a distraction.

But this time Tom didn't follow his mentor's advice. He went ahead and married his Edwina with wonderful, lifelong results.

For the next two summers, Edwina accompanied Tom to Macon. He worked at the *Telegraph* and she tried to fit into a community that was foreign to her. For a girl from North Georgia, the hot Macon summers were nearly unbearable. She had no friends and nothing to do. And the sulfuric stench from the paper mill south of town never seemed to leave the air. Although she grew to love

Peyton and the others at the papers, she never quite recovered from her first negative impression of Tom's hometown.

The summers weren't easy for Tom either. He was assigned to a number of what he saw as thankless tasks. One year they had him selling subscriptions in the outlying counties. He knocked on door after door after door, smiling and talking fast because he knew he had only about a minute to make the sale. Out of every twenty doors he approached, he was lucky to sell one subscription. Then he spent some weeks in the composing room. The crew there was unionized and he couldn't touch or do anything. All he could do was watch. Although he didn't explain it to Tom, Peyton believed if a person was going to run a paper, he had to know all facets of the business.

When Tom was in his last year at Harvard, Edwina saw a newspaper article about a new program President Lyndon Johnson was starting in 1965. The White House Fellowships were designed to bring twelve to fifteen young men and women to Washington from various professions. There at the White House they would be provided with firsthand experience in government, so that they could return to their chosen fields much better prepared to understand the role of the federal government in everyday life. Edwina wanted Tom to apply.

Tom liked the idea, but didn't feel free to pursue it. He fully expected to return to Macon after leaving Harvard and begin his career with the *Telegraph and News*. Still the White House Fellowship program sounded so exciting and worthwhile that he wanted to give it a try. It would only delay his return to the *Telegraph and News* by one year.

As he always did when considering an important decision, Tom talked to Peyton about it. Had the publisher demanded he come back to Macon, he would have done so without another word. He owed Peyton Anderson and the paper too much to defy his wishes. But Peyton gave his okay for Tom to apply for the fellowship. It may have not been the most enthusiastic okay, but he didn't say no.

While he waited for the decision from the White House, Tom again spent the summer at the *Telegraph*—this time in the circulation department delivering newspapers to carriers in the roughest section of town. While his Harvard Business School classmates were going off to $50,000 or $75,000-a-year jobs, Tom was getting up at 2:00 A.M. every morning, climbing into a white Telegraph van, picking up bundles of morning papers and driving to Unionville to meet his carriers. The carriers, all young boys, were supposed to be waiting at the pick-up point at 6:00 A.M., but it was a rare day that all of them showed up. It seemed there were always one or two absent. When Tom would call their homes, their mothers would tell him the boys were sick. Then he'd deliver those routes himself.

Armed only with a flashlight, he'd follow the routes in the van, searching for house numbers and tossing papers onto porches before sunrise. Too many times he overthrew the porch and the papers landed in the bushes. Then he'd get out with his flashlight, search through the underbrush until he located the paper and toss it on the porch where it belonged. More often than not, this activity roused the interest of the neighborhood dogs and they'd chase him all the way back to his van.

Collections were sometimes more difficult than deliveries. They were made in the afternoons and too often the subscribers wouldn't pay the carriers. Tom would go with the boys to try and collect the money, only to find that the people had moved or said they never meant to subscribe to the paper in the first place. This left the young carriers—eight, nine, or ten years old—without their money. When that happened, more often than not Tom would pay them out of his own pocket. He felt they deserved that much for being willing to get up and go to work at daybreak.

Some people might have resented being put in such a menial position, but Tom never asked why. He just did the job. While he didn't complain, Tom didn't enjoy his work that summer. Although he loved everything about the news side of the business, he had little fondness for circulation and advertising.

Peyton finally explained to him why he thought it was important that he do these jobs. "You always need to sell, service, and collect. Tom, those are the rules. You need to sell the paper, whether it's advertising or a subscription. You need to service your customers. That's picking it up and making sure it's not in the bushes, but on the porch. And you need to collect the money."

Peyton didn't really expect that Tom Johnson would be accepted into the White House Fellowship program. The competition was stiff and as the selection process progressed, Tom was the third regional finalist from the Southeast. However, when all the decisions were made, he was selected—the only person to be chosen from the South.

It was an extraordinary year for Tom and Edwina. Tom worked in the White House press office for Bill Moyers, and during that time, he and Edwina developed a relationship with President and Mrs. Johnson. The president may have first been drawn to the young man because he was a Southerner and a Georgian. Some of President Johnson's closest friends were from Georgia, particularly Richard Russell and Carl Vinson. He was also fond of Peyton Anderson. Whatever the reason, by the end of that year, President Johnson was not ready for Tom Johnson to leave the White House. He asked him to stay on as a member of the staff. Tom explained that he couldn't do that.

"Mr. President, I have a binding obligation to return to Macon. I have a binding obligation to Mr. Anderson to go back."

Like most people in his position, the President was not accustomed to being told no. He tried another approach.

"What if I ask Peyton if he'll let you stay here and continue to work for me?"

"Mr. President, I really can't urge you to do that. I'm under a commitment to return. Peyton sent me to the University of Georgia, sent me to Harvard Business School. I have to go back."

But President Johnson wasn't about to give in. In July 1966, he wrote Peyton asking his permission for Tom Johnson to stay on at the White House.

Tom feels a strong moral commitment to return to Macon because of everything you've done for him. His conscience will not let him walk away from that commitment. I'm proud of the way he feels and his integrity, but I believe he has a great opportunity here to make a significant contribution. This place has a way of stretching one's capacity, especially if he's young and eager.

I have told Tom that I would like for him to stay on if he could do so without breaching your confidence and faith. I know him well enough now to know that his sense of loyalty to you and his profound appreciation for your help in his life are overriding. He is torn between knowing that I need him and his desire to honor your confidence. I wanted you to know this and also to say that if you feel you could spare Tom Johnson, his country and his President need him.

Peyton was deeply disappointed, but he wrote back, giving his permission:

Dear Mr. President:

What opportunity could I offer Tom Johnson that could compare with that you mention in your July 28th letter? I feel he is the one to be considered and while we may have some small part in his education and experience, that knowledge should be used where it would be most rewarding to him and our country.

I am sure you would have had much less interest in him if he didn't possess the sense of loyalty he has demonstrated. I think he is outstanding in every respect.

Copy of my letter to Tom Johnson is enclosed. I think it is clear that he cannot afford to refuse the opportunity of your offer. He can live up to any expectancy you may have of him. It is now your responsibility to see that he gets that chance.

I would be glad to have him back here at any time, but I believe the experience and exposure in the White House, on your staff, will give him the greatest opportunities any young man could get.

Then Peyton added a postscript that was vintage Anderson: "How about that judgeship for our good and able friend, J. Elsworth Hall, Jr.? Copy of file on this is attached."

So Tom Johnson went to work for the President—as assistant to the press secretary.

Later that year Peyton was invited to Washington for an afternoon meeting with President Johnson. The objective of the meeting was to discuss the political situation in Georgia and the President's image in the Southeast. Peyton was excited about the invitation and also looking forward to having lunch with Tom Johnson in the White House mess at noon.

The meeting was scheduled for Thursday, May 19. Peyton had been in New Orleans that week and only arrived back home on Tuesday night. Wednesday was full of meetings and catching up on all that had happened while he'd been away, but he was confident that he could get to Washington in plenty of time. He had a reservation on the train from Atlanta to Washington, which he considered a "sure" method of transportation. Since Kat was spending some time in New York, he had arranged to meet her in Washington late Thursday afternoon. They would then take the Crescent train from Washington back to Atlanta—a relaxing, stress-free trip.

Wednesday had turned stormy and Peyton drove to Atlanta that afternoon in heavy rain and the tail end of a tornado. He boarded the Southerner at Terminal Station and sat back and relaxed in his sleeper compartment, confident that everything was well in hand. However, they traveled only two or three miles before the train stopped for what the passengers were told was "a freight switching."

Unworried, Peyton had dinner, then returned to his compartment, got dressed for bed and began reading a newspaper. In fact, he read two newspapers. The train still hadn't moved. He was now growing concerned. He pulled on some clothes and went to find a conductor. That was when he learned that there had been a wreck farther north on the line.

"But everything will be fine, sir," the conductor assured him. "We're waiting for a Seaboard crew to come and take the train on another route, up through Athens and Lula to Greenville. You should only be five or six hours late arriving in Washington."

Since that would put Peyton in the capital well past the time for his meeting with the President, he realized he had to change his plans. He was man accustomed to working around circumstance and felt sure he could master this situation. He fetched his bag and left the train, stepping down on a deserted downtown Atlanta street at midnight. He lugged his bag along until that activity brought on an attack of angina and he had to stop and find his nitroglycerin.

A bus came rumbling into view and he got on, alighting several minutes later near Terminal Station. He found his car in the parking lot and headed for the airport where he purchased a ticket on an Eastern flight that was scheduled to leave at 3:45 A.M. and arrive at Dulles at 5:15. Satisfied that adequate arrangements had been made, he went back out to his car to relax and read and wait until flight time.

A little more than an hour later, he noticed fog rolling into the area and realized this might be a problem. The first flight was canceled, but he changed his reservation to a later one that would put him in Washington around noon. Then, having a few hours to wait, he went to a pay phone and started trying to find a motel where he might get a little sleep before his 10:00 flight. Once again, he had no luck. There were no vacancies to be found.

At that point, Peyton surrendered to what seemed to be the inevitable. He decided he simply wasn't meant to go to Washington that day. He got back in his car, drove home to Macon and, at 6:00

A.M., called Tom Johnson to let him know he wouldn't be meeting with the President that day.

"I did all I could except get a charter plane," he explained. "Had I done that I would still have been without sleep and I didn't cherish the chest pains I was having."

However, he still wanted to share his observations with the administration. The next day, he wrote Tom Johnson a five-page, typewritten letter giving him his opinions on the state of national, as well as Georgia, politics.

Tom Johnson was promoted to assistant press secretary in 1967 and deputy White House secretary in 1968. When he was made one of eight special assistants to the President in 1968, he'd reached the highest rank that could be achieved on the White House staff.

Peyton received another White House invitation in 1968. This time the trip to Washington was accomplished without a hitch, and he and Kat attended a black tie dinner hosted by President and Mrs. Johnson on the occasion of the visit of the Prime Minister of Barbados.

In April 1968, Lyndon Johnson surprised the nation by announcing that he would not be seeking reelection, and Tom Johnson wrote to Peyton about that and his own future.

"I have told the President I will stay with him until he leaves office if he wants me to. After January, I must make another decision. You have been my most trusted counselor now for more than five years. It is to you that I want to turn first for advice and judgment." Coca Cola, the Hearst Corporation, CBS and Westinghouse had all approached Tom about working with them.

Peyton answered a week later. "There are many wonderful companies in our country. Good people can make working conditions excellent and pleasant. I'd say at your age you would want to see an opportunity to get to the top." He stressed the scarcity of privately owned businesses and reminded Johnson of what would await him in Macon.

> I firmly and unequivocally believe that any person owning a newspaper or a part of one should have to pay for it. Gifts of newspaper stock have generally produced second generation irresponsibility and not been good for the area served by the newspaper. I think I have provided for a realistic ownership plan, which I will be glad to outline for you.
>
> There is a definite spot here for you, but I think you have to evaluate it in relation to other prospects and your 'rathers'. You must decide what is best for TOM JOHNSON.

Tom stayed on at the White House through the end of the term. President Johnson asked him to accompany him back to Texas when he left office. Once more, Tom consulted with his mentor.

This time Peyton was blunt in voicing his opinion. "I know a decision so important to you is hard. Of course, I'm prejudiced, but a 'Former President' is a 'Past President'—and Tom Johnson doesn't want to live in the past. The years in the White House are memorable ones, but the future is ahead."

But Tom felt a deep loyalty to the president. He finally decided his course of action. In November 1968 he wrote what was a very difficult letter to Peyton:

> I guess it was out on Columbus Road that I first developed a burning ambition to rise above my situation. And you helped by providing opportunity for it to be channeled into a first-rate education. That drive is still in me today, seeking new horizons and new challenges—trying to be more than a sideline observer or Monday morning critic, but desperately seeking to be involved, to help shape things rather than tear them down as so many young people are doing today.

So in January I hope to move on to a new frontier. I do so with a prayer that you will understand. For a period of six months to a year, I expect to be Executive Assistant to President Johnson in Austin. In this capacity, I hope to help the President through his transition back to Texas.

He listed several projects that LBJ was interested in beginning—the presidential library, the LBJ School of Public Affairs, speaking engagements, and books to be written—projects in which Tom Johnson would be deeply involved. "After the time in Texas, I am not sure where I will go. I had thought of asking you to hold open the possibility of my returning there one day. But that would not be fair to you. Wherever Edwina and I go, our lives will be guided by the imprint you placed on us many years ago."

Tom Johnson never did return to the *Telegraph*, but he and Peyton never lost touch.

Denny McCrary was another Macon boy with a connection with Anderson. He began a paper route for the *Macon News* in the early fifties, then delivered papers for the *Telegraph* for three more years. His ambition all through school had been to attend the Naval Academy and, when Peyton was approached on the boy's behalf, he gladly wrote a letter of recommendation for him. McCrary received Senator Walter F. George's principal appointment and entered the school in 1956.

Peyton was involved with alumni affairs at the Academy and served on the Board of Visitors, so he made several trips a year to Annapolis. No matter how busy he was on these visits, he always made time to see the Middle Georgia boys who were in residence there. Denny learned not to be surprised to get a call in his room saying Peyton Anderson was downstairs to see him. He'd rush down to the first floor reception room and spend some time with the older man, catching up on news from home and reporting on his own progress. It was comforting to talk to someone from Macon who was looking out for him.

In the years after the Academy, McCrary and Anderson touched base every now and then. McCrary went on to take a commission in the Air Force and then attended Harvard Business School. He made a career in the real estate and resort business, spending nine years on Hilton Head Island in South Carolina and twenty-eight years at Sea Island, Georgia. He retired in 2003 as president of the Sea Island Corporation.

Jim Wooten grew up in Macon where he attended Willingham High School and was editor of the yearbook his senior year. His teacher and yearbook advisor was Betty Lou O'Keefe. She was determined that the young man go to college, but he explained to her that he would have to work a while and save some money before that would be possible. His parents were divorced and money was tight. But Miss O'Keefe wouldn't let the idea go.

Early one Saturday morning in the spring of 1963, she took him to meet with the admissions director at Mercer University. O'Keefe was a persuasive and determined woman. Before they left the office, Wooten had been admitted to Mercer. Following his teacher's advice, Jim applied for some small scholarships and received one from the Winn-Dixie Corporation. It was enough for two quarters' tuition and he started school in the fall with the goal of entering the ministry after graduation.

While the scholarship paid tuition, Jim still needed money for living expenses. So he got a job at the Mercer bookstore after school and worked Saturdays at the *Macon News*. In those days, the *News* put out a Sunday edition that was, for the most part, the product of a group of college students. They came in on Saturday mornings, worked from seven to twelve o'clock, and put out the paper—sometimes without a single full-time staffer in the newsroom. It was an extraordinary experience for the students.

Jim loved working at the paper, and the bookstore was not a bad way to spend his afternoons, but even with two jobs, he didn't have enough money to pay for an education at Mercer. When his scholarship ended in the spring of 1964, he dropped out of school and went to work full time on the assembly line at the Blue Bird Body Company, a school bus manufacturer. He planned to save his money and set his sights a bit lower than Mercer in order to get a degree.

But he continued to work on Saturdays at the *News*. As summer approached, managing editor Jay Trawick offered him a full-time job for the summer. He took it and saved every penny he could. He applied to Middle Georgia College, part of the statewide university system, and was accepted for the fall quarter.

In late August, Peyton Anderson called Wooten into his office. He told him he'd heard good things about him from Jay Trawick. He then explained that he had started awarding scholarships to a few promising young people, including Tommy Johnson. Finally, surprising the young man, he said he'd like to do the same for him.

Jim Wooten gratefully accepted offer. It made a significant difference in his life. The money from Peyton Anderson would cover tuition and books for all of his undergraduate years. He attended Middle Georgia College that year as planned, working every weekend and through the summer at the newspaper. The next fall, he transferred to the University of Georgia. While he was in Athens, he was a full-time employee of the *Athens Daily News*, but he still commuted to Macon every weekend. His summers, too, were devoted to working at the Macon newspaper.

Like Tom Johnson had before him, Wooten came to realize that the *Macon News* was providing him with as much an education as the University of Georgia. Jay Trawick, Bill Maynard, George Doss, and Joe Parham, among others, were generous in teaching him what they knew. He couldn't have asked for a more thorough grounding in the newspaper business.

Although Peyton never in any way suggested that he expected it, Wooten always planned to return to the *Macon News* as soon as he graduated from college, but the draft and the Vietnam War intervened. He entered the Army as soon as he got out of school in

1967. When he was discharged in 1971, Peyton had sold the papers. While the obligation he felt was to Anderson himself, Wooten still interviewed with the *Macon News*. But when he told editor Joe Parham that the *Atlanta Journal* had offered him a job paying considerably more than the *News* could, Parham advised him to take it.

Jim Wooten went on to spend over twenty-five years with the *Atlanta Journal and Constitution*, with an early break to work for *US News and World Report*. To this day, he believes he owes Peyton Anderson a debt that cannot be repaid.

11

Grandchildren, Black-eyed Peas, and the Sale of a Newspaper

Every year, Kat or Peyton wrote to their distant grandchildren and asked what they wanted for Christmas. By 1968, the Bleibtreus had moved to California. Joshua and Jason both sent their Christmas wish lists to their grandparents.

Joshua's letter read: "Dear Pate, I've thought and thought about Christmas and keep coming back to this advertisement and I finally figured out that this is what I *really* want." He enclosed an ad for a Monza racing set.

His younger brother also enclosed an advertisement—for a Javelin Rocket Kit, priced at $6.95—in the letter addressed to his grandmother. "Dear Big Kat, I love you very much. I miss you a lot. Since you wrote and told me to pick something for Christmas, here is what I want. Josh is going to help me fly it. We have already picked a place to set it off. Sincerely, Jay."

Peyton took care of procuring the rocket kit himself. On *Telegraph* stationery he wrote to the Centuri Engineering Company/Educational Products Division: "Enclosed is my check for $6.95 covering one complete Javelin Rocket Kit, which my grandson Jason Bleibtreu says he would like for Christmas."

Peyton was not a man who paid much attention to different social or economic levels. He was just as comfortable chatting with the guys in the composing room as he was managing a meeting in the boardroom. And he cared about all of them. At Christmastime, he sent big boxes of Washington State apples to each employee. To some of their children, those who had no other association with the publisher throughout the year, those apples made Peyton Anderson synonymous with Santa Claus.

Every New Year's Day, Peyton hosted a party at which he served the traditional fare of hog jowls and black-eyed peas. Friends, family, and a good number of employees were invited. Over the years it became known as Peyton's Pea Party. And for *Telegraph and News* employees the invitation was in the nature of a command performance. Peyton was a believer in the superstition that eating hog jowls and black-eyed peas brought luck and money for the coming year. Conversely, failure to do so would bring disaster to the person and, possibly by association, to the *Telegraph and News*.

One year, city editor Jim Chapman and his wife got tickets to the Gator Bowl football game in Jacksonville. Since they were from that part of the country, they were very excited about going back for this special event. There was only one snag—they'd miss Peyton's New Year's Day party. It was up to Jim to tell his boss they wouldn't be there.

Peyton wasn't pleased when he heard the news, but going to the game was obviously important to the Chapmans and he knew he wasn't going to talk them out of it. "Okay," he finally said, "if you promise me you'll eat hog jowls and black-eyed peas wherever you are, we'll let you go this time."

Chapman promised. He and his wife had a good time in Florida. They visited with family, saw the Gator Bowl and even managed to eat hog jowls and black-eyed peas on New Year's Day. Jim was afraid not to. He didn't want there to be any way *he* could be blamed if there was a crisis at the paper that year. And for the rest of the time he worked for Peyton, he never again made plans for New Year's Day.

Peyton continued to be very active in the American Newspaper Publishers Association. He was a member of numerous committees and served for several years on the Board of Directors. Whether theirs was a weekly publication or a daily paper in a big city, there was one thing that all newspaper publishers had in common—they all had to deal with the powerful unions that represented their employees.

There was always the threat of a strike in the world of newspaper publishing. While Peyton never had one on his watch, there were some close calls. Once, during contract negotiations in the early sixties, one of the union negotiators, frustrated at not getting what he wanted, threatened to call a strike. The room got very quiet. This was serious business. Peyton stared at him silently for a minute, then his face relaxed into a pleasant expression and he shrugged.

"Well, if you want to strike, go ahead and strike. It's perfectly okay with me. I've got about $100,000 lying in the bank not doing a thing. If you want to strike, it won't bother me in the least."

There was no strike and eventually the negotiations produced a settlement.

However, the employees of a print shop a few doors up the street from the paper did go out on strike. They were picketing, carrying signs and shouting slogans as they marched back and forth in front of the business. Gradually the area of their demonstration widened to include the sidewalk in front of the Telegraph Building. Peyton stalked outside and confronted them. "Nobody is on strike here," he told them. "So walk up there! Don't walk in front of my building."

Juanita Jordan never planned to go to work for the *Telegraph and News*. The mother of a two-year-old child, she had a part-time job driving a school bus and wasn't interested in doing anything more at the time. Then a friend who worked in the bookkeeping department of the newspaper asked for a favor. A coworker was having surgery and would be out for quite a while. Could Juanita fill in for six weeks? It would just be basic clerical work.

Since it was summer and there were no bus driving duties to perform, Juanita agreed. A couple of days later, she went to work for Harold Wood, treasurer of the corporation. She was competent and pleasant, and got along well with the other employees. After the woman she'd been replacing returned to work, they pressed her to stay on.

"Just stay another couple of weeks," Wood asked. She agreed and then, two weeks later, the same request was made. "Just stay on another two weeks." Juanita didn't mind working and the extra money was welcome, but she knew that summer was nearly over. The time was coming when she'd have to leave the paper and she told Harold Wood that. Soon afterwards, Peyton Anderson sent for her. She'd met the publisher—he came to the bookkeeping department from time to time—but she couldn't imagine why he wanted to see her.

"What does he want?" she nervously asked Harold Wood.

"Well, I don't know."

"What have I done wrong?"

Wood shook his head. "I don't think you've done anything wrong."

She made her way to Anderson's office, afraid of what was coming. Anderson was an overpowering personality and she dreaded having him be angry with her. She thought and thought, but couldn't come up with anything she'd done that might have upset the man.

Then he did the last thing she ever expected—he offered her a job. His secretary Jeannette Gausch was seriously overworked, he said. In addition to her usual duties, she oversaw the operation of Drinnon's Photography and the helicopter business. He wanted Juanita to come to work as Jeannette's assistant.

Juanita didn't exactly jump at the chance. "I don't really want to give up my school bus."

But Peyton was used to getting what he wanted. "Would you work in between the times you drive the bus?"

She thought for a moment, then said, "Well, I would work from maybe ten till two."

"Okay, why don't you plan to help Jeannette from ten till two?"

And that settled it. She found she enjoyed the work and learned more than she'd ever expected from the publisher. He was flattered at her interest and happy to tell her all about the newspaper industry.

By the fall of 1968, much of the country was humming Beatles tunes and watching Jacques Cousteau's undersea explorations. Peyton Anderson was growing tired of the responsibility of running two newspapers. He'd hoped that Tom Johnson would return to Macon one day and eventually take over the business, but that didn't appear likely now.

"The three dreams of a newspaperman—to own his paper, its building, and its press—I'd already had," Peyton would say later. "I'd done it all. Typos ran me crazy; there were labor problems. I didn't have the youth and I was getting fat and lazy."

So he started looking around for a likely buyer. It wasn't as simple as publishing an ad in the paper and waiting for someone with the purchase price to show up. The newspapers had been a part of his life for as long as he could remember and the people who worked there were family to him. He felt a tremendous responsibility—not only to those employees but to Middle Georgia as well—to make sure the papers continued in the tradition in which they'd been started.

Peyton had come to know John and Jim Knight of Knight Newspapers, Inc., through his membership in the SNPA and the ANPA. Their friendship had grown over the years. He and Jim Knight had become especially close—often fishing and hunting together. The Knight Corporation owned newspapers in Ohio, North Carolina, Michigan, and Florida. Anderson liked what he knew about their operation and was pleased when they showed interest in purchasing the *Telegraph and News*.

His old friend Alvah Chapman had gone to work with Knight in 1960 after he and Mills B. Lane, Jr., sold the Savannah papers. It was Chapman, then executive vice president of the corporation, whom the Knights chose to negotiate with Peyton for the sale of his newspapers. On the table were not only the *Telegraph* and the *News*, but also the Milledgeville weekly paper and Drinnon Photography. After a number of meetings, Peyton and Chapman had reached a general agreement that the sale would go through, but no firm decision about the terms had yet been made.

Chapman was in the publisher's Macon office one January morning and they were hammering out the details of the probable sale. They had tentatively agreed on $19 million as the purchase price when the telephone interrupted their negotiations.

Calling was Ed Estlow, CEO of Scripps-Howard. With no pretense of small talk, Estlow then and there made Peyton an offer of $20 million for the papers. Although there was no concrete deal—not even a handshake—with Knight at that point, and even though he might have been able to use this new offer as leverage to get more money from one side or the other, Peyton didn't hesitate.

"No," he told the caller, "I've already made a deal."

He believed that Knight had the same sense of responsibility to the communities they served that he himself had always felt toward Macon. He was also impressed with the news and editorial content of their papers. They were, in short, the best-qualified organization he knew to carry on the *Macon Telegraph* and the *Macon News*. So he sold the papers and Drinnon to Knight Newspapers for $19 million and a seat on their board of directors. At 1:15 P.M. on 25 February 1969, ownership of the Macon papers passed to Knight Newspapers and Peyton found himself retired. Letters of congratulation poured in from all over the world.

The sale of the papers prompted his long-time secretary Jeannette Gausch to retire. Once more, he called Juanita Jordan in for a meeting.

"Jeannette is retiring and I've taken an office in the Charter Medical Building. Would you go with me and help me look after my investments?"

"Well...I don't want to work full time."

"I know, I know. Ten till two. Will you come?"

On June 2 when Peyton moved out of the Telegraph Building to the fourteenth floor of the Charter Medical Building, Juanita Jordan went with him.

Along with Juanita, Peyton invited a second person to come to work for him. Doc Smith had retired from the papers in 1964, after rising through the ranks to circulation manager and, eventually, a place on the board of directors. He and Peyton had developed a close relationship during his time at the paper and he regarded the younger man in an almost parental way. He'd never wanted to retire in the first place and jumped at the chance to go back to work. Doc's exact duties were never actually spelled out. He ran errands, handled the mail and bank deposits, and did a little bit of everything else.

When Julia Northrop retired from the *Telegraph and News* in 1965, she was eighty-one years old. Her husband had died some years before, but Miss Julia was still quite active and, more than once, terrified her friends and relatives by climbing onto the top of her house to repair the roof. She also continued to cut her own grass and once missed a birthday party being planned for her by Bill Ott when a rock flew up from under the lawnmower and injured her leg. Bill wrote her a note saying she was the only person he knew that would throw rocks at herself to avoid having to come to her own birthday party.

Miss Julia died on 17 July 1970. Her funeral service was held at St. Paul's Episcopal Church and she was buried in Rose Hill Cemetery.

12

Shields and Investments

What happened to the families of police officers and firefighters who were killed on duty? Not months later when the insurance payments had been made, but immediately afterwards? That question troubled Peyton Anderson in the late sixties. He pondered it for quite a while, discussing it with friends and colleagues and researching the solutions other communities had found. In 1968, he decided to form the Shield Club, modeled on an organization of the same name in Florida. He and twenty-one other civic leaders, including Bob Dunlap, Ed Sell, and Bert Struby, incorporated the club, then began recruiting members.

Peyton sent out letters that read, in part:

> For some time I have been concerned about the families of law enforcement officers and firemen in our area who may be killed in the line of duty. These people's families have a need for immediate money until pension funds become available.
>
> A group of us got together and are incorporators of THE SHIELD CLUB, set up to do this job.
>
> Basically, THE SHIELD CLUB, when a law enforcement officer or fireman is killed in the line of duty in Bibb County, will immediately present a check to the widow for $1,000. We then investigate the indebtedness of the deceased and decide which portion of their indebtedness should be paid by the club.

In many cases, it is possible to pay off all indebtedness, such as mortgage on house, car notes and loans.

Each year THE SHIELD CLUB members will meet at a sensational party, building friendships and making membership especially desirable.

They planned for 100 members, with individual dues set at $300 for the first year. No politicians or city or county officials were allowed to join. Only private citizens were accepted as members.

Twenty-five people attended the organizational meeting of the Shield Club on 29 April 1968, at the Macon Elks Club. Bud Hobbs of the Pompano Beach, Florida, Shield Club spoke to the group describing his organization's formation and activities. They also elected officers at that first meeting. Peyton Anderson was chosen president, J. V. Skinner vice president, James H. Sheehan treasurer and Ed Sell, Jr., secretary. The membership in 1968 was eighty-eight.

The Shield Club proved to be a popular and effective organization. Mills B. Lane, Jr., thought so much of it that he offered to pay half of the original membership fee for any C&S Bank director who joined. Twenty of them took him up on his offer. Their first annual party, a black tie affair with dinner and dancing, was held in November 1969 at the Idle Hour Country Club.

The club grew steadily and eventually expanded their purpose. Although their main concern was still providing for families of slain officers and firemen, they included as a secondary function the honoring of officers for exceptional service.

Mason Zuber had been a nine-year-old paperboy at the *Telegraph* in the 1920s when he first met Peyton Anderson. At the time, all Mason knew about the dapper young man in the circulation department was that he was the publisher's nephew. But Macon was a small town and the two crossed paths a number of times over the years. The insurance agency where Mason later worked and eventually owned, was only a few blocks away from The Telegraph

Building. The two men met at various business functions from time to time. However, it wasn't until Mason and Miriam Zuber purchased a house on Lake Sinclair across the lake from the Andersons that the two couples got to know each other and soon became close friends.

During the summers, both couples spent almost every weekend at the lake. As soon as he arrived, Peyton would raise the flag at his house. This notified the Zubers and others that he and Kat were in residence and ready to greet guests. When they weren't communicating by signal flags, they used CB radios. No telephone lines had yet been run to the small lakeside community in the late sixties.

The Andersons often had dinner guests at the lake. Peyton cooked late—ten or eleven at night—and a typical meal would be steaks, corn on the cob, and butter beans. He once had oysters flown in from the Gulf of Mexico and hosted an oyster roast there in the yard.

Their friendship eventually extended beyond Lake Sinclair. Peyton and Mason fell into the habit of having lunch together once a week in town. They'd drive out to Lowe's Cafe on Gray Highway where Peyton loved the chicken and dumplings. And Kat and Miriam took several European vacations together.

Like Peyton, Mason loved giving and getting presents. A friendly contest soon developed to see which of them could find the most unique gift for the other. Peyton once presented Mason with seven neckties, a different day of the week printed on each one. And when he and Kat visited Switzerland, they brought back a heavy iron cowbell, complete with a brightly colored woven harness, for their friends. The Zubers had the bell hung outside their lake house.

The most remarkable gift was probably the one that Mason found for Peyton in South Carolina. It was a huge piece of driftwood; at least six feel long, carved and painted to resemble a buxom mermaid. He found it in a shop in Hilton Head and drove home with it sticking out the window of his car. Peyton loved it. He immediately christened the mermaid Suzy and displayed her prominently in the lake house where many a glass was raised in her honor.

Peyton always enjoyed gift giving, especially when it allowed him to share a new invention with someone. When color televisions became available, he bought one for himself and one for Laura Nelle's family. Every time a new camera model was put on the market, Peyton bought several. He gave some away and kept one for himself. He took pictures of everyone and everything. After a number of years, there were so many photos that they finally catalogued them and stored them in a big, metal file cabinet.

The microwave oven was another appliance that excited him. In addition to the ones he purchased for himself and Laura Nelle, he gave one to Doc Smith and his family. When Doc brought the new appliance into the house, Vera regarded it with suspicion and declared she'd never use it. However, within months, she'd learned to prepare a number of dishes in the microwave and would never have voluntarily given it up.

One year, a truck pulled up to Ed Sell's house. It was a delivery from Peyton—a barrel of live Maine lobsters. For a short time, the Sells weren't sure what they were going to do with their gift, but Peyton came to the rescue. He threw a party at their house and cooked lobsters for everyone.

Peyton traveled frequently and Doc and Juanita were left alone for the much of the first months they were in the new office. Juanita oversaw the work of the carpet layers and painters, making decisions on her own because the boss was not available. Peyton returned to a decorated and fully furnished office.

Juanita continued with the schedule she and Peyton had agreed upon. She was in the office from ten till two and drove the school bus mornings and afternoons. The schedule suited her, but Peyton grew restive with it. One afternoon, he called her in to talk about it.

"Look," he said, "I know your husband is number one with you, but I don't like being number three. The school bus is number two right now and I'm number three and I don't like it." He made her a generous offer to work for him full time and she gave the school board her notice. From then on, she was supposed to be in the office from nine to four every day, but those hours were more suggestion than reality. When Peyton was in town, she rarely left for home on time. He loved to talk and he was interested in everything. It wasn't unusual for him to wander into her office just before four o'clock and start regaling her with stories about the day's events or some gadget he'd discovered. Once begun, the talk could go on for an hour or two.

Anderson was not a self-centered man. Everyone and everything around him fascinated him. Any time Juanita went shopping and brought her purchases back to the office, he couldn't wait to see what she had. If she didn't immediately share the information with him, his curiosity prodded him until he had to ask what she bought and where she found it.

There was one kind of shopping, however, that he didn't like. He still disapproved of anyone in Macon shopping for clothes in Atlanta. When Juanita did so, on occasion, he would scold her. "You made your money in Macon," he'd say, as he had preached over the years, "spend your money in Macon."

Doc Smith and Juanita Jordan got along famously. Doc so admired Juanita's wisdom that he started calling her Sage. Doc's wife Vera often referred to their relationship as a love affair, but one she approved of. In fact, Vera was almost as fond of Juanita as her husband was. The two women became good friends, sometimes meeting downtown for coffee or lunch.

Doc worked from nine to one every day and one of his regular duties was to take his and Peyton's checks to the bank and deposit them. He joked with Vera, "I always wonder what would happen if I deposited my check to Peyton's account and his to mine." He laughed. "But before I get there, I decide I'd better not do that."

Doc adored his wife. As he was quick to tell anyone who'd listen, she was the only woman in the world for him. When Vera told him something, it was gospel. One morning Juanita arrived at the office and, as was her habit, made a pot of coffee. She poured herself a cup and, when she took the top off the sugar bowl, found a note in Doc's handwriting that read: "Use less sugar and stir like hell." It turned out that Vera had told him a person could lose ten pounds over the course of a year by simply eliminating the sugar from coffee and he was passing on that advice.

Peyton's business was now investment, and he took great interest in every part of the process. He was a very hands-on investor, carefully researching any proposed purchase and rarely putting his money into a corporation where he didn't personally know the people involved. He decided to teach his staff what he had learned. He sent Juanita to a class at Merrill Lynch and, in the early seventies, he sat her and Doc down and told them he was going to give them some real-life experience.

"I'm going to give each of you $25,000. You can invest it any way you want. That's the best education you can have."

Juanita and Doc were flabbergasted and more than a bit nervous. They wanted to do well, but weren't really sure where to start. After some discussion, they decided to invest in Coca-Cola and Eastman Kodak. Juanita called a broker she knew at Merrill Lynch and told him what they planned. He was not encouraging.

"Well," he said, "Merrill Lynch is advising clients not to buy Coca Cola at this time."

They told Peyton what the broker had said. "It's your call," was the only advice he gave them.

That sent Doc and Juanita back to square one. After more talk, they concluded that the broker must know more about it than they did, so they bought only Eastman Kodak. Consequently Coca-Cola stock increased significantly in value. Later it doubled, tripled and eventually split. Juanita complained to Peyton that the man at Merrill Lynch had given them bad advice.

He wasn't sympathetic. "Let that be a lesson to you. All that man does is read and make his decisions. You can read just as good as he can. He's a salesman. You read and you make your own decisions. That's good experience."

Soon after that, Juanita asked his advice about investing in Citizens and Southern Bank stock. Later the same day, Peyton's friend William Fickling, Sr., stopped by the office.

"Bill," Peyton said, "Juanita wants to know what you think about C&S stock."

"Well, I don't know about C&S, but if you got some money that you don't have to have a return on right now, Charter Medical is a pretty good investment."

Peyton did invest in Charter, but Juanita and Doc hesitated. Although Fickling had recommended it, they knew that his son ran the company and were reluctant to put too much faith in his recommendation. He might, they reasoned, be too optimistic about the stock because it was his son's business. Once again, they didn't invest and once again, the stock in question went up, eventually doubling and splitting. Peyton, of course, made quite a tidy profit on Charter Medical.

The two beginner investors finally put their money into Citizens and Southern National Bank stock because it seemed safe. While their investments did well enough, they'd have made a much greater profit investing in either Coca-Cola or Charter. However, the experience they gained was priceless.

13

A Yacht is Christened

There had been a lot of good times at the Lake Sinclair house, but after his retirement, Peyton longed more and more for the open ocean. So during the summer of 1970 he purchased a fifty-three-foot yacht from the Hatteras Corporation. He and Kat went to North Carolina to pick it up, taking Rags Parrish and their grandson Reid Hanson with them. They cruised down the Carolina coast and, on June 10, the night of their fortieth wedding anniversary, Kat christened the boat "Peyton's Place II" by breaking a bottle of champagne over the bow. Later that night, Peyton commemorated the occasion by giving his wife a diamond bracelet.

The four of them sailed down the Intercoastal Waterway and, when they reached Sea Island, Georgia, Reid was put ashore to meet his mother and return home. The three adults continued their trip south, ending up in the Florida Keys. Peyton and Kat had visited the Ocean Reef Club in Key Largo several times and liked it. They arranged to dock their boat there and, soon afterwards, purchased one of the club's condominiums.

This was the life Peyton had been born to live. He loved the sun, the water, and the tropical lushness of the place. He was on his boat or at the condo every minute he could manage. He was driving a diesel-powered station wagon at the time and had a second fuel tank installed in the car so that he could drive from Macon to Key Largo without having to stop for gas. Kat wasn't as fond of the boating life as her husband was. Her health wasn't good and she often preferred to stay home near family and friends when Peyton went south.

The two did spend Christmas on the boat that year. They dined in many of the area's excellent restaurants, took advantage of the club's two golf courses, and took their boat out onto the ocean for day trips up the coast. But Peyton wanted to go farther and for longer stays. He came to the conclusion that the boat he'd purchased was too small for what he wanted.

The next year, he quietly began looking around for a larger yacht. He finally located one that he believed would suit him in Providence, Rhode Island. In November 1971, he flew up and had a look at it. Built specifically for watching yacht racing, it was sixty-nine feet long with spacious observation decks. Below decks were two staterooms plus the crew's quarters, luxuriously furnished and rich with mahogany. Peyton purchased it then and there and called Kat to tell her about his new boat and invite her on its maiden voyage.

She joined him in Rhode Island a few days later. They hired a crew and the next day sailed into New York City Harbor. However, they struck a log on the way in and damaged the hull. Peyton and Kat spent several days in New York, waiting for the repairs to be made. They made the most of their impromptu visit, dining well and shopping. When the boat was ready, they went back aboard and traveled with it to the Florida Keys.

Now Peyton owned two yachts—one more than he needed. He considered selling the first, but decided instead to donate it to the International Oceanographic Foundation. It was an organization he'd first learned about several years before and he admired the work they were doing in south Florida.

With Lawrence E. Dunbar as the captain of the new boat, also named Peyton's Place II, Peyton was ready to do what he loved best, and he invited those people he cared about to enjoy the boat with him. Blanche and David Redding were frequent guests, as were Ed and Pree Sell and Mason and Miriam Zuber. Peyton's invitations could be impulsive and he was known to schedule guests' visits quite close together. Once Mills Lane had sailed with him for several days. They planned to return to Ocean Reef on Saturday and Lane would be going home from there. Peyton called Ed Sell and asked if he and Pree would like to come down for a cruise. When Sell accepted, it was arranged that they would meet at Ocean Reef on Saturday. When they docked in Key Largo, Lane was hesitant to leave. He'd had such a good time that he wanted to extend his visit a few more days, but Peyton's Place II was already booked. Lane was put ashore and Ed and Pree were brought on board.

Peyton had a reputation for being a generous man. Although constantly approached for donations, he was particular about where his money went. He didn't fall for hard luck stories, but willingly helped people he believed deserved that help.

He kept his membership at St. Paul's Episcopal Church although he rarely attended services there. When a specific need arose, such as repairing the roof, Peyton would step in and take care of it. However, he wasn't interested in providing day-to-day support for the church. He believed the attending members should take care of the operational costs.

He continued his support of local charities, including the Shield Club, and was a member of the President's Club at Mercer University. That association, however, ended abruptly in 1970. Opposition to the Vietnam War was at its height and the country seemed in danger of being torn apart. Peyton's patriotic anger erupted when anti-war activist Jane Fonda appeared at Mercer on November 17. She was part of a six-month lecture series that included Jack Anderson, Bernadette Devlin, and Julian Bond.

Peyton was furious. He called the president of the university and demanded that the person responsible for Fonda's appearance be fired. He was astonished when the president explained that the professors who arranged the series could not be fired because they had tenure. That very day, Peyton sent a letter resigning from the

President's Club and, from then on, refused to support any school that granted tenure to its employees.

Tom Johnson continued working for Lyndon Johnson into the early seventies in spite of the numerous job offers that came to him. Peyton strongly believed that he should move on with his career, preferably with Knight Newspapers. He urged him to do so in several letters and also lobbied the Knight management to make Johnson an offer. The offer was made, but Johnson turned it down. He felt a strong loyalty to the former president and refused to leave him.

"In good conscience," he wrote to Peyton, "I must see my obligations discharged. I can't run out now, although I know it may result in my losing the best opportunity of a lifetime."

Peyton's return letter reflected his disappointment.

Sorry you felt you had to stay on there instead of joining KNI September 1. I feel you had a great opportunity with KNI. LBJ will pull everything in the book to keep you there. Of course he needs you, but I feel your opportunity will be more rewarding as being yourself, rather than basically identified with a memorial project.

My love to Edwina, Tom and Christa,

Bestest, Peyton.

The two men had kept up a correspondence since the time Tom had attended Harvard. They exchanged information about their lives and work, and often drifted into the political and philosophical arenas. When Tom sent him *A Nation Can Be Libeled, Too*, an analytical article about the Pentagon Papers by Louis Nizer, Peyton wrote back:

Louis Nizer has hit the nail on the head about the Pentagon Papers fiasco. I was in Switzerland when all this happened. My reaction then, as it is now, is that it is much ado about nothing. I don't see what was gained in publishing a so-called 'study' and relate it to actions.

On every issue and prior to a decision, all facets should be explored. The decision is a result of weighing pros and cons. Decisions are what count, not the study. You can study yourself to death and nothing happens until action is taken.

There is no such thing as rights without responsibility in exercising those rights. Freedom of speech and freedom of the press are no exceptions.

In September 1972, Peyton wrote Tom, dwelling on politics and the future of the newspaper business:

You have seen politics at its best and its worst. In it, you are a king one day, a bum the next. There is no job security, no real reward for conscientious performance. The reward is for being popular, not being necessarily constructive.

The trend as I see it today is towards public ownership, newspapers have gone that route. I predict most important newspapers will be publicly held, like the other big corporations in 20 years.

During the CBS national news broadcast on the evening of 22 January 1973, a filmed report from Vietnam was shown. When the camera returned to Walter Cronkite, he was holding a telephone to his ear and saying, "Yes, Tommy, I'm on the air now..." He then turned to look into the camera and announced that he'd just been informed by Tommy Johnson, aide to Lyndon Johnson, that the former president was dead.

Two weeks later, Tom wrote to Peyton.

I lost one of the best friends I ever had when President Johnson died. He went away in much the same fashion as he traveled as President, without much advance notice to anybody.

The highest tribute ever paid me by either President or Mrs. Johnson was when Mrs. Johnson got to San Antonio and was told by the doctors that LBJ was dead. She called me to say 'Tom, we did not make it *this* time. Lyndon is dead. I will need you at my side during these next difficult days and weeks—just as you always were at Lyndon's side.'

My other friend, still well and healthy I hope, is Peyton Anderson. I hope these next few days and weeks will permit us opportunities to see more of each other. Besides, *you* made all these past 8 years possible.

Tom also shared the news that he'd been offered an editor's position.

Peyton was pleased at the prospect of Tom's new job: "The Dallas Times-Herald job should be a natural for you."

14

Hoi Toi and Angels

The seventies was a decade of upheavals. The Vietnam War raged, the Senate held hearings on the use of Agent Orange, and it seemed protest demonstrations were springing up everywhere, for any and every reason. The anti-war rallies drew bigger and bigger crowds. In California, Native Americans occupied Alcatraz Island. Liberation and consciousness-raising were the catchwords of the day.

In 1970 Katty and John Bleibtreu moved their family to Chile to study with teacher and philosopher Oscar Ichazo, founder of the Arica School. Although Chile was an unstable country at the time, the Bleibtreus never felt they were in any danger. During their time there, a fourth child, Sarah, was born to the couple. After a year out of the country, they returned to the United States and settled in California where they both taught the Arica philosophy.

Deyerle and Russell Hanson separated in 1971, later divorcing, and Russell was absent from his children's lives for several years. It was only natural that thirteen-year-old Reid and his grandfather grew closer during that time. Peyton often took the boy hunting and fishing, and the two spent hours discussing the future. Reid was doing well at Macon's Stratford Academy and was involved in the swimming program there. He confided that his ambition was to follow in his grandfather's footsteps and attend the Naval Academy, with the goal of becoming a Navy pilot. Peyton was flattered and encouraged the boy in his dream. He encouraged him to attend a good prep school, believing that it was a key element in getting into the Academy. In 1971, Reid was accepted to the Bolles School in Jacksonville, Florida.

When Reid came home for the summer vacations, he often spent the day at the Oakcliff Road house where Kat put him to work in the yard. She also had him climb up on the roof and clean out the gutters. It was hard labor by anyone's standards, and Kat was very particular about having the chores done correctly. Then, in the middle of the day, the boy was expected to clean up and join her for a sit-down lunch in the big dining room. He enjoyed those meals, flattered that she treated him like another adult, ready to discuss any and all subjects with him.

In the summer of 1972, Peyton took Reid to Annapolis to see the Naval Academy. Peyton's good friend and Academy roommate, Rags Parrish, went along with them. They were given a tour of the campus, had lunch at the admiral's table, and dinner at his personal residence. Reid, a typical fourteen-year-old, took all this in stride. He assumed everybody visiting Annapolis had the same experience. He didn't realize until he was older that the treatment they'd received there was reserved for a very few, very special people.

It wasn't necessary to be part of a charitable institution to be a recipient of Peyton Anderson's generosity, as an unsuspecting woman in Durham, North Carolina, learned in 1973. Kat had experienced some problems with weight gain in her later years and went to Duke University to take part in their famous rice diet. When her treatment was complete, Peyton went to North Carolina to bring her home.

Waiting outside the hospital's Business Office to settle his wife's account, he noticed a woman in the waiting area with a black plastic box strapped to one wrist. Peyton couldn't share an elevator ride with another person without talking to them, so it wasn't surprising that he struck up a conversation with her.

"What's that on your arm?"

She smiled without any real humor. "The doctors make me wear it. It's supposed to convince my brain that my back doesn't hurt."

"Does it work?"

She gave a weary shake of her head. "No, That's why I'm here. I'm going to have surgery. This is my last chance. I've already had eight or nine operations. I'm just about broke. I've only got enough money for one more try, so this is really my last chance."

When Peyton paid Kat's bill, he quietly arranged to pay the bill of the woman with the black box.

"On one condition," he cautioned the Business Office clerk. "You are not to tell her who paid it."

Typically Peyton didn't mention this remarkable act of kindness to anyone. No one in Macon would have ever known about it if a letter hadn't arrived in his office four months later. Juanita Jordan opened it as she did all the mail. It was from the woman whose bill he'd paid at Duke University Hospital. She wrote that it had taken her three months' persistence to get his name from the people at the hospital. Her thanks was heartfelt and profuse.

A very personal honor was awarded to Peyton on 27 April 1974. His portrait, done in charcoal by Macon artist Houser Smith, was unveiled at a reception in the lobby of the Telegraph and News Building. Kat and Deyerle were present along with about fifty of his former employees. Alvah Chapman, president of Knight Newspapers, Inc., flew in from Miami to attend the party and praise Peyton for his decision to sell his papers to Knight.

"He knew what he wanted to do with the newspapers because his life was in it and his mark will be here for a long time in the future."

Then Peyton spoke a few words to the group. He told them that he felt good about selling the papers to the Knight group. "Their theory of publishing is in line with my own. And their treatment of this company is in line with the way I tried to treat you when I was here." Then he laughed. His closing line was vintage Peyton. "Thank you for hanging me here today."

Although he was no longer publishing a newspaper, Peyton was still vitally interested in the events of the day and his counsel was valued by business and political leaders of the time.

For many years he corresponded with Senator Herman Talmadge. Their topics ranged from government spending to gun control to unemployment. Peyton was never shy about voicing his opinions and and clearly expected Talmadge to make changes and get things done in Congress. In 1977, the Senator tried to explain the problems he encountered: "I certainly share and understand your concern about the economy and wasteful and excessive federal spending programs. I have only one vote in the Senate and I have thus far been unable to translate my single vote into the kind of corrective action you and I, and most Georgians, would like to see."

Throughout his career, Tom Johnson had consulted Peyton about his plans and opportunities and carefully considered his advice. Whenever the opportunity was presented to mention Peyton's tremendous contributions to him and his career, he made sure he gave the former publisher the credit he deserved. After Johnson took what he considered to be his first real job—editorship of *The Dallas Times-Herald*—he wanted to repay Peyton for all that the older man had invested in him. He suggested repayment of the money first, but Peyton would have nothing to do with that idea, refusing to take a penny. So Johnson found another way.

With Edwina's encouragement, he contacted the University of Georgia and established the Peyton Anderson Scholarships. He had only a small amount to contribute in the beginning, but that amount would grow considerably over the coming years.

On 20 September 1973, the University of Georgia News Service issued a press release in which Dean Warren K. Agee of the School of Journalism announced "the establishment of the Peyton T. Anderson Scholarships, honoring the former longtime publisher of the Macon Telegraph and News." The scholarships would be presented annually by W. Thomas Johnson, Jr., executive editor of the Dallas Times-Herald and a former protegee of Anderson. Nominees for the scholarships had to be entering freshmen and Georgia residents who planned to major in news–editorial journalism. The scholarships continue to this date, still supported by Johnson and supplemented by grants from the John S. and James L. Knight Foundation.

Peyton was deeply touched by this gesture and wrote Tom in October 1973: "Dear Tommy, I am humbled by your setting up the scholarship in my name. I feel undeserving of the honor you have bestowed on me. Many thanks to you for what you mean to me. I'm mighty proud and humble."

He signed it as he did many of his letters "Bestest, Peyton."

The same day, he wrote to Dean Agee:

Tommy Johnson has honored me beyond what I deserve. I just wish I knew others like him to assist.

It is a small thing to provide meager funds for a person's education, but to be fortunate enough to see a man like Tommy develop is what makes life really worthwhile.

I hope in selecting recipients of the scholarship he has set up, you will find at least one who can be as rewarding to Tommy as he has been to me.

The Dallas Times-Herald was named one of the five best newspapers in the South under Johnson's leadership. Soon after that, he was scheduled to receive a prestigious award from the National Jaycees. He invited Peyton to be there for the ceremony, but Peyton declined the invitation. "Florida and warm weather is calling loudly," he wrote, "and I have a strong urge to leave the rain and cold to enjoy a little sunshine."

Johnson kept trying to give credit to Peyton. He wanted to be able to introduce him to his friends and the influential people he now knew, to have everyone meet the man he believed was responsible for his success. He invited Peyton and Kat to spend a weekend at his Dallas home with several other guests, including Ladybird Johnson. But Peyton sent his regrets, saying that his directorships kept him very busy.

In December 1975, Johnson was selected as the new publisher and chief operating officer of *The Dallas Times-Herald*. In his letter sharing the news, he tried to explain how much of the credit he believed should go to Peyton: "You instilled in me a burning desire to achieve. You provided the means for me to acquire that most essential of all assets: knowledge—and you championed a nobody from the wrong side of the tracks from sports stringer and West Macon circulation substations through the White House." He advised that, effective in January, there would be three additional scholarships bearing Peyton's name at the University of Georgia, bringing the total to four. "They'll remain there as long as I'm able, as a living tribute to Peyton T. Anderson, my benefactor and friend."

Peyton spent more and more time on his boat, but he didn't neglect his business when he was at sea. Juanita was his eyes and ears when he was away from the office. She kept up with the stock market and his portfolio's performance. She read the *Wall Street Journal* every day, making note of anything that might interest him. Then, every day or two, Peyton called her on a ship to shore radio to get the latest news.

The first time he used that device, his assistant found the experience unsettling. As she was bringing him up to date on the status of his investments, he interrupted her.

"Now remember, this is open air way and everybody can hear what you're saying."

That knowledge made Juanita terribly nervous. She wasn't sure that she even had any secrets, but now began to wonder what, if anything, she could safely tell him. After every such conversation, she was exhausted and her desk was a shambles because of her feverish search through the papers for items she could share with Peyton on that open line.

One morning when Peyton came in the office, Juanita noticed he had a tiny pin shaped like an angel on the shoulder of his suit coat.

"What is that?"

He smiled. "Nobody can resist talking to you when you've got an angel on your shoulder in the elevator."

Not long after that, Tom Johnson was in town and stopped by for a visit. He noticed the angel himself. In a way, that angel came to define for him a lot of Peyton's personality. Even though the publisher was wealthy and had great influence in the community and in publishing circles, there was an angelic quality to him. It shone in his warmth, his humor, and his caring for others.

"He never, ever publicized his financial gifts to me or any of the others he gave to," Johnson said years later. "Those of us who were lucky enough to be the beneficiaries proudly told others about Peyton, but he never did that or wanted any public recognition."

When Peyton was in the office, he liked to keep busy. During slow times he always found ways to amuse himself. He'd challenge Doc or Juanita to a game of TV tennis or hockey. If they weren't available, he'd play his pachinko game, a kind of desktop pinball machine that he'd received as a gift.

Juanita and Doc soon became extensions of Peyton's own family. When Juanita had surgery in 1974, Peyton insisted on providing her with round-the-clock nurses for three days, even though she assured him that it wasn't necessary. He did the same thing some years later when she was hospitalized in an automobile accident. Like it or not, she had nurses with her every minute of the time.

Whenever he spent a weekend at the lake house, he usually cooked, and he'd bring the leftovers to the office to share with Doc and Juanita. Peyton loved onions and peppers and spicy foods of all kinds. Once he brought them barbecue that was so hot neither of his employees could eat it. When he was busy on the telephone, they slipped out and gave it to the architects next door.

Summer was a time of bounty and Peyton loved fresh vegetables. Sometimes he'd buy huge quantities of them at the Macon Farmers' Market. Six bushels of butter beans or black-eyed peas was a common purchase. He'd have them shelled at the market, then bring them to Juanita who'd take them home, blanch them, and put them in bags to be frozen. She'd keep half and return the rest to Peyton.

Christmas was a holiday that brought Peyton Anderson much enjoyment because one of his greatest pleasures was giving gifts. Rather than send cards, Peyton sent gifts. His list contained nearly 300 names and he spent a great deal of time each year deciding upon just the right present. Catalogues would begin showing up in the mail in September. He and Juanita would debate for weeks about the most appealing items, and then they'd order one of each of the top eight or ten choices so that they could get a good look at them before the decision was made.

Once the gift was selected, the appropriate number was ordered. Box after box would arrive at the office. The chore of wrapping them all fell to Juanita. Peyton also sent oranges and apples to close friends and family, and there were always twelve to twenty recipients each year of ready-to-eat turkeys and dressing. During the week before Christmas, a day rarely passed without a delivery from Peyton to Laura Nelle's house.

Although Peyton and Kat gave the grandchildren numerous expensive presents, Peyton also loved finding small, silly gifts for them. For Christmas of 1980, each grandchild received a wristwatch that played "Dixie."

While he was remarkably generous, Peyton did expect his gifts to be acknowledged. If a recipient didn't send him a thank you note, that name was struck off next year's list.

Any time he had trouble coming up with the perfect Christmas gift, he could always fall back on Hoi Toi. It was in a tiny shop in

Hong Kong in 1961 that Peyton first discovered a small figurine of a buddha, with a huge belly and a big smile. This, he learned from the attached card was Hoi Toi or the Laughing Buddha. In other Asian cultures, the figure was known as Hotei or Pu-Tai. The card gave the following account of how the statue had come to be:

> Many hundreds of years ago, men went on foot to fight wars and were often gone for years at a time. So it was with a small village in China. The men packed up and went away, leaving only one male in the village to protect the women and children. That person was Hoi Toi. When, years later, the soldiers returned, they found the population of the village had dramatically increased. There were many young children and new babies. The men were furious and erected a statue of Hoi Toi in the center of the village. To make him the object of ridicule, they gave the statue a huge belly and a silly grin. Hoi Toi is believed to bring good luck and great bounty.

Peyton loved that story and he loved the statue. He began collecting the figures and even incorporated the image onto his stationery. He used the Hoi Toi imprint on numerous Christmas gifts. He sent figurines, of course, but there were also trays and plates and vases adorned with the emblem. In his office, photo frames and lampshades displayed Hoi Toi stickers.

Most people thanked him nicely for the gifts, but a few wrote to advise that they didn't worship Buddha, although they appreciated the thought. He got a particular kick out of those letters.

Peyton loved receiving gifts as much as he did giving them. A couple of years after he began sending out Hoi Toi gifts, Blanche and David Redding turned the tables on him. For Christmas, they presented him with a huge, very heavy, five-foot-tall Hoi Toi statue. He kept the gift in his office where it was quite a conversation piece.

Another time, Mills Lane sent Peyton a replica of a ship's figurehead, complete with a buxom woman's upper body. Peyton wasn't quite sure what to do with it. While he was deciding, he hung it out of the way behind the office door. Every morning, as regular as clockwork, Doc Smith came into the office, opened the door, closed it and hung his hat behind it. It was a routine that never varied until the morning Doc came face to face with the figurehead.

"What the ...! What *is* that thing?"

Juanita was laughing so hard that she could barely tell him.

Every Christmas Juanita and Ed Sell got together to try and come up with the perfect gift for the man who had everything. They'd usually get him a gadget or a gag gift of some kind. Juanita would do the shopping and Ed would do the buying.

On his birthday every year, Juanita either baked a cake or had one made for him—the more unusual the better. One year she presented him with a cake in the shape of a gray elephant with bright pink hindquarters. On it was written "Happy Birthday Peyton" and at the bottom of the cake were the words "PAE Anyone?"

This was Juanita's acknowledgment of one of Peyton's favorite stories. A local lawyer friend of his was in the habit of carrying large amounts of cash at all times. When the curious asked why he did so, the lawyer informed them, "If I see a pink-assed elephant and want it, I'll be able to buy it."

Finding gifts for Peyton was always a challenge. He was a man who, while he might not have had everything, could certainly have bought anything he wanted. Yet he loved getting presents. For one of his birthdays in the late seventies, Juanita came up with a one-of-a-kind gift. She designed and had made a quilt with twenty squares, each one representing a milestone in his life. As the date to present the quilt grew closer, she became more excited. Finally the day came. She and Ed Sell walked into his office and handed him the quilt she'd spent so many hours planning.

"Happy Birthday!"

He unfolded it and then spread the quilt across his desk, silently examining each square. Finally he took a deep breath.

"Thank you."

Juanita was terribly disappointed. Usually Peyton was excited receiving gifts. He gushed, he laughed, he enthused. But all he'd done in accepting the quilt was to mutter two words. It wasn't until later that Ed Sell explained to her that Peyton had been so touched that he was, for once in his life, at a loss for words.

15

Guiding the Next Generation

It's not always easy to maintain close relationships with grandchildren, but Peyton worked hard at it. As the years passed and they all moved out of state, he relied more and more on letters to keep the ties strong.

Reid Hanson's dream of becoming a pilot died when he learned that his eyesight wasn't good enough. With that dream gone, he also lost interest in the Naval Academy. However, he continued swimming and in 1974 achieved All-American status in that sport. He wrote to his grandfather declaring his determination to get a swimming scholarship to college.

Peyton's reaction was pragmatic:

> Remember, swimming is great and a fine way to parlay it into an education, but first you want to get the education along the lines you want and that can be most rewarding to you in life. As I recall the age 22 is about the last of the great swimmers. After that you have to get into something to house, clothe and feed you and others you may acquire along the way. Get your sights on what you want to do to make a living in your life and get the education to prepare for that just as you have prepared yourself for the swimming honors you have amassed.

Reid did get a swimming scholarship—a full scholarship to the University of Georgia. During his time there, he and Peyton corresponded frequently. Many of Reid's letters asked the older man's advice and Peyton was always ready to share his opinions and experience.

> You have had a rough time over the past several years emotionally. You have had a great disappointment in one you had love for. I have tried to be available, understanding and advising you when you wanted the advice. I am glad you think I have made the grade and can warrant your confidence. I hope you will always feel you can level with me. I will never intentionally let you down. Try me out when you feel like it.

As a boy, Reid had found it more comfortable to express himself to Peyton in letters rather than in person. But, during his college years, he lost that self-consciousness and enjoyed the face-to-face give and take. When he visited his grandparents, he and Peyton would stay up late, talking about everything imaginable.

One Christmas his grandfather sensed that Reid was troubled. After Kat went to bed, he opened a fifth of Jack Daniels bourbon and he and his grandson sat down to drink it. That was when Reid admitted he was struggling with a problem. He was dating a young woman and couldn't decide whether or not to propose. Peyton didn't tell Reid what to do. Rather, he recounted some of the lessons he had learned in life. By the time they went to bed, the bottle was empty and Reid had decided against marriage.

Jason Bleibtreu wrote to Peyton from Chile where he lived for a year with his parents, and then from the Marvelwood School in Connecticut. Jason, who was known as Jay, visited his grandparents as often as he was able and especially enjoyed fishing trips with Peyton. As Jay's interest in photography grew, his and Peyton's roles reversed a bit. In later years, more often than not it was Jay sending Peyton slides and photos instead of the other way around.

On his eighteenth birthday, Kat and Peyton sent Jay a sizable check—the same gift they gave their other grandchildren reaching that milestone—and Peyton wrote the accompanying letter.

"A few years back the good old US of A started recognition of 18 year olds as having reached maturity and assumed responsibility of manhood. It has been my good fortune to be able to give some recognition to my grandchildren who have reached 18. We are mighty proud of you and love you dearly."

Adam Bleibtreu's contact with his grandfather had a marked increase as he reached college age. He was a student at the University of Southern California and had become excited about taking some television production courses. When Peyton learned his grandson was interested in television and the media, he insisted that Adam get in touch with some people he knew in the business. He encouraged him at every turn.

Three days before he graduated, Adam sent a letter to Kat and Peyton in which he thanked them "for all that you both have done for me. Thanks to what you and Jack and Helen [his paternal grandparents] have done, I have had the chance to go to college. By providing for my education, you have given me the freedom to do what I want with my life. I can think of no finer gift. With love always, Adam."

Adam's brother Josh was arguably the most independent of all the grandchildren. When his eighteenth birthday arrived in May 1975, he was living on his own in California. His grandparents sent him a check and Peyton wrote: "Been a long time since I have heard from you. In the meantime, you have attained the new legal age of manhood—18. Your mother tells us of your independence and taking care of yourself financially. You must be doing great on the car rebuilding and training from what she says. We miss hearing from you and hope we'll have a visit with you one of these days."

Josh did visit with them in Florida the next year and several times after that.

When Laura Hanson was sixteen she began attending the Rocky Mountain School in Colorado. In 1976, she enrolled at the University of Oregon and the change of environment was a shock. "I feel like an anonymous face walking around," she wrote her grandparents.

Peyton's answer was empathetic: "The trouble with big schools is you are just a number. I understand Oregon has about 15 thousand students. I thought 2,400 a lot at the Naval Academy back in 1492. Feeling ignored is terrible. I often say 'Give me hell, but don't ignore me.'"

Laura wasn't sure where she wanted to go with her life during her first years in college. When she changed her major to Fine Arts in her sophomore year, Peyton wasn't pleased.

"Where is this acting and art jag going to get you?" he wrote. "Sooner or later you're going to have to support yourself." As he had several times before, he urged her to take typing. "Typing will be the most valuable talent you possess, no matter which way you go. What is the matter, is it just too routine to interest you?"

Laura eventually took his advice and sent him a typed letter, advising that her classes were going well and that she had typed the letter herself on her "new second-hand typewriter."

He wrote back, typing *his* letter himself: "Be damned if you can type so nicely and accurately I'll have to give it an old try and bang this out on—as you describe it—an antiquated Royal. So you can snicker and say 'though late in applying myself, I have at last gotten where I can show up that old grandfather in typing—as well as other things.' I'm trying to say I'm proud that you are putting things in order."

Peyton Anderson Hanson was Deyerle's and Russell's second son. When he reached high school age, his grandfather encouraged Deyerle to send him to a prep school, just as she had Reid. When she agreed, Peyton enthusiastically joined her in the search for a school that would be suitable for his grandson. He finally concluded that Darlington School in Rome, Georgia, was the right place for the boy. Deyerle had remarried by this time and her new husband, Larry McNair, was a graduate of the same school.

Peyton wrote to Gordon Bondurant, president of Darlington and expressed his admiration of the place. "It is my belief that education involves physical and mental discipline. Your aims seem to project this same feeling. I have a high regard for your graduates I have known. I hope Peyton will be as outstanding and will have the same rewarding experience at Darlington as I did at Riverside. His scholastic and extra curricular activities are almost as bad as mine before going off to school."

In 1978, Peyton Hanson was enrolled in The Darlington School. Later he attended Santa Barbara College before being accepted at the Brooks Institute. His grandfather was pleased:

"Mighty proud of you and hope you will let me in on your learning, activity, ambitions and thoughts. You are a great guy and I love you."

16

Farewell to Peyton's Place II

The social life in South Florida was active. Peyton joined the prestigious Key Largo Angler's Club and was also a member of the International Oceanographic Foundation's Society of Benefactors. The ANPA held meetings at Ocean Reef, the SNPA's annual conventions usually took place in Boca Raton, and Knight Newspapers, which became Knight-Ridder in 1975, was headquartered in Miami and hosted a number of functions there. Peyton was often mentioned on the society pages of *The Miami Herald* where he was once described as "silver-haired, crewcut Peyton Anderson, retired Macon, Georgia publisher and bon vivant."

When he was faced with something he couldn't have, it only made Peyton Anderson want it more. The man whose mother had once described as "the hardheadedest boy I've ever seen", wanted to belong to the Card Sound Golf Club. Located on the northern end of Key Largo, it was a very small and very exclusive club. Their membership was limited to a couple of hundred members and, when Peyton decided he wanted to join, he learned that the membership list was full. No one else would be allowed to join until there was vacancy. Peyton wasn't ready to sit back and wait for that to happen. He was used to getting what he wanted no matter how hard he had to go after it.

Card Sound became a crusade. He talked to every member he knew. He pushed and prodded until finally an exception was made for him and he became a member. After all that, he never once played golf at Card Sound. It had been the challenge, not the golf course, which was important to him.

In the late seventies, Peyton's Pea Party was moved from Macon to the Key Largo Angler's Club. He invited his neighbors and new acquaintances in Florida, but issued invitations to family and friends back home as well. One year he flew Doc and Juanita down on the Citizens and Southern Bank jet. They helped him put on the party and even decorated a Christmas tree on the yacht.

When Peyton entertained on his boat, he liked his guests to have keepsakes of their visit. He had David Redding at Macon Tent and Awning make him a quantity of laundry bags, similar to small duffel bags. They were navy blue, with white piping and a white drawstring at the top. At a local embroidery shop, the words "Peyton's Place" and the Hoi Toi figure were stitched on them in white. Every guest was urged to take a bag home with him.

Of course, Peyton's gifts weren't limited to laundry bags. He also gave visitors fishing equipment or items of clothing. Once, when Laura Nelle and Dan O'Callaghan were staying on board for a week, they drove up to Cedar Key for some shopping. There Peyton purchased Lilly dresses for Laura Nelle, because he knew she liked the brand, and brightly-colored sports coats for Dan.

"We didn't know if he was being generous or was just ashamed of what we were going to wear," Nelle joked.

Cruises on Peyton's Place II were full of things to see and do. At sea, there was fishing and snorkeling. In port, Peyton and his guests made sightseeing excursions, shopped and dined at the best restaurants. One of Peyton's favorite stops was the International Oceanographic Institute where, he said, he would show his guests "how man came out of the ocean."

Peyton still pinned the angel to his shoulder, but his attire in Key Largo was much less formal than what he'd worn in the office. In addition to the angel, he acquired another accessory. On occasion he'd wear an earring in one ear, giving him a decidedly piratical look.

Grocery shopping was as much an adventure in Florida as it had been in Macon. One year he and Kat invited Juanita to go along on a trip with them. The cruise to Chub Cay in the Bahamas was expected to take about two weeks, so the three of them went to a grocery store in Ft. Lauderdale to buy provisions. Peyton insisted that they each have a buggy and kept piling items into them. By the time they reached the check out line, all three carts were very full and they had enough provisions for two or three months.

In 1976, Captain Dunbar hired a young woman named Taffy Folsom as his first mate. She quickly became a favorite of Peyton and Kat and everyone else who sailed on Peyton's Place II. Taffy did most of the cooking while they were at sea and quickly learned that she could never put too many onions in a dish for her boss. Peyton was so fond of the vegetable that he'd bring big bags full of Vidalia onions from Georgia for use in the galley.

Taffy had other duties as well, of course. She cleaned the staterooms, went shelling for guests, and was an experienced diver. In the Florida waters, lobsters could only be caught legally during certain seasons. Peyton took to calling them squirrels and, when lobster was out of season, would casually ask the mate, "Taffy, do you suppose we could have squirrel for dinner?" She'd know exactly what he meant. Minutes later, wearing a mask and fins, she'd go over the side and dive to the bottom in search of lobsters.

The meals that Taffy cooked for Peyton and his guests were generally simple fare—fish or steak, salad, and potatoes. However, one year she got a chance to stretch her culinary horizons. Kat Anderson took a cruise with three of her female friends. On that trip, Taffy got to show her talent in making soufflés, quiches and delicate sauces.

In 1977, Tom and Edwina Johnson moved again, this time to Los Angeles where Tom was to become the president of *The Los Angeles Times*. He had kept a photo of Peyton on his desk through the years, but now wanted a new one. "Peyton, I want an inscribed photo from you for my new LA Times office," he wrote. "It will go alongside Edwina and the children." When Peyton sent the picture, it was inscribed: "To Tom Johnson. My greatest pride is in your many outstanding accomplishments."

That same year, Peyton lost two dear friends. Doc Smith died in February, leaving the office a quieter, colder place. His beloved Vera continued to live in their house until 1987 when she had a stroke. Her daughter Berma realized that Vera could no longer live alone and she called the one person her dad had trusted to make hard decisions. Juanita heard her out, made one telephone call, and found a comfortable, loving rest home for her. Juanita and Berma took Vera there the next day.

In July 1977, David Redding died of complications from open-heart surgery. Even though he'd been ill for some time, his family was devastated. His son David had recently become engaged and the wedding was planned for October. It was heartbreaking to think that his father hadn't lived to see him marry. In early autumn, David went to see Peyton. When he married Janie Ford, Peyton Anderson was standing by his side as his best man.

Kat's health was still troublesome and she and Peyton decided they needed to find someone to live in the house and help out with the daily routine. However, before that would be possible, they needed more space. It was time to add on again. This time they had a spacious two-bedroom apartment built on the back of the house.

When Jake McDonald retired from the *Telegraph* in the late seventies, Peyton hired him and his wife Vee and moved them into the new apartment. Vee did the cooking and Jake ran errands and tried to keep up with the never-ending work in the yard. It was an arrangement that seemed to suit everyone.

As the decade drew to a close, Peyton spent less and less time on his yacht. He couldn't avoid the realization that it was expensive. He'd sit in his office for hours calculating with pen and paper and then announce to Juanita just how much it cost him every day to run the boat and keep a crew when he wasn't even there. He finally decided he had to get rid of it.

In the fall of 1978, he put Peyton's Place II on the market. There were no immediate takers, so during Christmas of that year, he gathered as many of his family as possible to celebrate the holidays at Ocean Reef. In addition to the boat, he rented several condos to accommodate everyone. The Bleibtreu clan was there, along with the Hansons and the O'Callaghans. When New Year's Day came, Peyton pressed everyone into service to help prepare hog jowls and black-eyed peas. He was expecting quite a crowd.

Taffy cooked on the boat while Laura Nelle did the same in one of the condos. She watched as Peyton started a big pot of ham hocks and water boiling. Then he added rice. Laura Nelle was sure he hadn't used enough rice. As soon as he left, she added more. And, a little later, she checked the pot and added even more. Soon the boiling water began increasing the rice's volume—to such an extent that she was afraid the dish had been ruined. Not wanting Peyton to know that she'd made a mess of his prized recipe, Laura Nelle began scooping the rice out of the pot. Since a garbage can full of rice would give her mistake away, she threw the excess out the back door. When it was time to serve the meal, no one, including the head cook himself, noticed that anything was awry.

The yacht still hadn't sold by February 1979 and Peyton was getting anxious to close that chapter of his life. He decided to donate it to the International Oceanographic Foundation, just as he had his first boat. On Valentine's Day, he and Kat flew down to Florida where they boarded the boat, packed up their personal gear and, as Peyton put it later, "had a beautiful run into Ft. Lauderdale." Kat flew back to Macon and the next day Peyton signed the boat over to the Foundation.

Jake McDonald had driven the Seville down to Ft. Lauderdale. He and Peyton rented a U-Haul trailer and hitched it to the car. Late that afternoon, after Peyton said good bye to Larry Dunbar and

Taffy Folsom, he and Jake headed for Macon in heavy rain. They'd planned to stop for the night at about 8:30, but found when they arrived in Wildwood, Florida, there were no vacancies at the local motels. When the situation was the same another hundred miles north, they decided to drive on through to Macon.

The weather was worsening. Soon they encountered snow, sleet, and freezing rain. Many of the bridges were iced over and their progress slowed to a crawl as they neared Macon. They finally pulled into the driveway of the Oakcliff house at 4:30 that morning and they were lucky to get home when they did. By daylight the roads from Middle Georgia north were covered with a sheet of ice and travel was impossible.

While Peyton must have surely felt some sadness at giving away the boat that had brought him so much pleasure, he wasn't completely unhappy. "I feel relieved to be free of the expense and responsibility of the boat," he wrote to his grandson Reid. "It will save me a hunk of money."

17

The End of One Story

Kat Anderson might not have been 100 percent healthy, but that didn't keep her from the traveling she loved. To celebrate her seventieth birthday, she took an Around Africa cruise. Sailing from Florida, she was installed in a stateroom on an upper deck of a luxury ocean liner. After crossing the Atlantic, she spent eight days in Kenya and Tanzania, and visited Delphi, Cairo, and Luxor.

Although he didn't go with her, Peyton took pains to see that her trip was safe and convenient. He contacted the Associated Press bureaus in every port she was scheduled to visit to let them know that Kat would be on the ship. Then he provided her with a list of the people at those bureaus she could call on for help. Several times he had fresh flowers delivered to her stateroom.

Kat didn't always travel alone. In 1979 and again in 1980, she took her daughters with her to Europe. It was during a car tour of England that Katty and Deyerle realized just how intelligent and knowledgeable their mother really was. The three had hired a car and a driver who also served as a tour guide. Kat sat in the front and chatted with him while her daughters relaxed in the back seat. They were primarily interested in historical sites and Kat had a list of places she wanted to see.

Two or three days into the trip, the guide mentioned to Katty that this trip was not a typical one. "I don't know whether you know this or not, but when I take most people around, I can go to the pub in the evening and drink," he said. "With your mother, I can't."

"Why not?" Katty asked, mystified. She knew that her mother would never have tried to tell the guide what to do in his free time. She soon learned that it had nothing to do with drinking and everything to do with pride.

"When we're talking about history, she'll *correct* me," he said, sounding slightly offended. "I'm a fairly well educated Englishman. I'm a graduate of Oxford. But I'll check and your mother's right—every time. I can't go to the pub in the evening. I have to study up for the next day's trip because your mother knows our history better than I do."

In early 1980, it was announced that Tom Johnson had been chosen publisher and chief executive officer of *The Los Angeles Times*, the largest newspaper in the country. His appointment was to be made official at the Editorial Awards Banquet in the ballroom of the Beverly Wilshire Hotel on March 7. Johnson desperately wanted Peyton to attend. This would be his opportunity to finally thank Peyton publicly for all he'd done for him.

Tom wrote to his friend and mentor: "If you can possibly make it, I want you in Los Angeles on March 5-6-7. Edwina and I will host a private dinner for you on March 6.

"This is one moment in my life where I want you here to share it, Peyton. Edwina insists that you come. It would mean so much to have you here."

And Peyton did consider going. He looked up flights to Los Angeles in his airline schedule and contemplated several that would have him arriving there on the 6th and returning on the 8th. But in the end, he decided against it, explaining to Juanita that Tom should be the one in the spotlight that night, not him.

He wrote to Tom:

The thought of any recognition of your ability pleases me greatly. You have exceeded all expectations anyone may have had for you. You have excelled in every activity and accepted and met every challenge. Nothing pleases me more than to see you recognized. You deserve it all.

For you to want me to participate with you is great for my egotism. You have done more than could be expected in the way you have always remembered me. The scholarships are enough in themselves.

I am most flattered you want me with you March 6 and 7. The arrangements really sound 'up town'. Why not just let me come out later when I can have a relaxed visit with you, Edwina, Wyatt and Crista. I'll enjoy it more than some big affair.

For some time I have had a date for a bass fishing trip March 4-9. It is with a group of close friends.

Think it over, Tom. Is it really important to you that I be in Los Angeles March 6 and 7? I don't react well in big crowds and parties, you know.

Bestest, Peyton

Johnson's star continued to rise. In 1990 he became president and CEO of Cable News Network and, in 1999, chairman and CEO of the entire CNN operation before retiring in 2001. Through it all, he never missed an opportunity to credit Peyton Anderson with his success.

Peyton was diagnosed with bladder and prostate cancer in 1981. He had surgery and then began a long radiation and chemotherapy treatment, but his illness didn't keep him from enjoying Christmas that year. It was a special one for him and Kat because they were able to gather their entire family around them in the Oakcliff Road house for the holiday. Peyton was in his element planning and booking flights for everyone coming from out of state. It was a wonderful time for all of them and, a few days after Christmas, Peyton took his grandsons on a hunting trip.

Perhaps the highlight of the holiday was that Peyton and Kat had the chance to get to know their youngest grandchild Sarah Bleibtreu better than they ever had before. Reid noticed this and mentioned it to his grandfather in a 5 January 1982, letter: "Thanks for a great Christmas. Two things really stick in my mind that I will always remember was talking to you that night after our first night out hunting and seeing you and Sarah talking outside in front of the fire at 1182 that Saturday night."

Like most fathers, Peyton still had trouble thinking of his grown-up children as adults. One evening when Deyerle was home for the holidays, she decided to visit an old friend. Her father was concerned about her driving after dark and told her so.

"I'll be fine," she told him. "I do it all the time and I'm careful."

He wasn't convinced. "You'll just get in trouble," he predicted, "and I'll just have to get you out of it."

She didn't get in trouble, of course, and Peyton was realistic enough to know that she and Katty both lived on their own and did it quite well, but he never got over the idea he had to look out for them.

Kat's love of gardening didn't diminish a bit, even though her health made it more difficult for her to take part in the activity she so enjoyed. She continued to oversee Jake McDonald's work in the garden. She was especially proud of her roses and in May 1982, she and Jake won a blue ribbon for them.

Later that summer, Jake himself became ill. He and Vee told the Andersons they were going to have to retire. But Jake thought he knew just the people to replace them.

Jake and Jack Eich had been friends for years. Eich, the service manager of a local Volkswagen dealership, had in the past jokingly told McDonald that he wanted his job. Now Jake informed him it was available. Jack's wife Sarah was recovering from arterial surgery.

Before her illness, she'd been a buyer for a clothing store, but her recuperation was going to be lengthy. She knew she wouldn't be able to go back to the store for quite some time. Jack and Sarah talked it over and thought the job with the Andersons might be just the thing for them.

Sarah and Jack were invited to the Oakcliff Road house to meet Kat and Peyton, one evening in late summer. Sitting and talking with the Andersons, the Eichs felt an immediate rapport. Although there were some things to consider—Jack's job, the house they owned, and their daughter Cathy who would be a senior in high school that fall—when Peyton made his offer, they accepted on the spot.

The Andersons gave their new employees a tour of the house. It was a spacious place, beautifully decorated. The kitchen itself was a work of art, and Sarah had never seen so many books in one house in her life. There were bookshelves in the living room, the library, the hallways, and the bedrooms. Kat even had a small book-lined study of her own.

"I've seen libraries with less books," Sarah told her husband on the way home.

The Eichs moved into the apartment with their daughter Cathy two weeks later. The apartment bore no resemblance whatsoever to servants quarters. The rooms were large and airy and filled with good pieces of furniture and a number of antiques. The sofa in the living room had been in Kat's family for over a century. When the Union army marched through Virginia, the McClures had moved that sofa from their home into the deserted slave quarters to keep it from being burned.

The official title given to the Eichs was "caretakers," but that description wasn't nearly broad enough. They handled a variety of responsibilities. Sarah oversaw the running of the house and hired people to come in and clean. Both of the Andersons were aware that she was still recovering from major surgery. Anytime she showed the slightest indication of becoming tired, she was encouraged to sit down and rest. Kat thought they should hire a cook, but Sarah was reluctant to do that.

"I don't know if anybody could please me," she said. "And I enjoy cooking."

After Sarah prepared a few meals for the Andersons, there were no further suggestions about hiring a cook.

The couple was responsible for administering the household accounts and the shopping. Jack maintained the grounds—both on Oakcliff Road and at Lake Sinclair—and the vehicles. He hired the workers he needed to keep the yard looking the way Kat wanted it to. However, she refused to let anyone but Jack cut, prune, or feed her beloved roses.

Kat and Peyton still traveled when they could. He liked hunting, fishing, and life at Ocean Reef while Kat preferred Europe and New York City. When one of the Andersons was away, the other often joined the Eichs for dinner at the kitchen table. On nights when they were both home, Kat would dress up for dinner and the meal would be served at the long table in the dining room. "We're going to do it right tonight," she'd tell Sarah.

Some times both Andersons were away, leaving the Eichs alone in the big house. It was on afternoons like those that Sarah would take a glass of tea into her favorite room in the house. The library was furnished with big, comfortable chairs, reading lamps, a fireplace and wall-to-wall books. There she'd curl up with a book for an hour or two of reading. Whatever her interest on a given day—mystery, art, biography, romance, gardening—there would be a book to suit it.

Life was more interesting for the Eichs, however, when their employers were home. The Andersons still enjoyed entertaining. They hired caterers for big parties, but Sarah and Jack handled the smaller gatherings. Peyton often returned from Florida with shrimp and oysters, and he and Kat would invite one or two other couples over for an oyster roast on the big barbecue pit in the side yard. His hunting trips sometimes resulted in a box of quick-frozen quail, which Sarah would prepare with wild rice. It was one of Peyton's favorite meals.

Cathy Eich began her senior year of high school soon after she and her parents moved into the Anderson home. She enjoyed living there. She was especially fond of Kat, who took an active interest in the personable young woman who had come to live on Oakcliff Road. Cathy had a part-time job at Eckerd's drugstore and got off work around 8:30 in the evenings. Her first stop when she arrived home was usually Kat's bedroom. Cathy kept her supplied with cigarettes and Cadbury chocolate from the pharmacy. After making her delivery, Cathy would get comfortable and she and Kat would talk. The older woman had been so many places and done so many things that her stories fascinated the schoolgirl. And Kat enjoyed hearing about the day-to-day happenings of Cathy's life.

After earning his undergraduate degree there, Reid Hanson entered the School of Veterinary Medicine at the University of Georgia. By spring of 1983, he was looking forward to graduation and marriage to fellow vet Laura Lawson. After the wedding they planned to move to New York where Reid would intern at the Cornell Veterinary Hospital.

In a March letter, he asked his grandfather to be best man at his wedding.

"You have been my closest friend all these years, have given sincere advice in good times and bad, have provided me the opportunities to grow, learn and develop my full potential, but most of all have always been there when I needed you."

Writing from Florida, Peyton explained that his health was poor and he would have to decline. He was still recovering from cancer surgery and chemotherapy. "Since then I have been going too strong—shooting, traveling, fishing and doing too much for a man near 76—and it has got to be a lesson." A couple of weeks before, he'd come down with a severe case of the flu and was still very weak.

The doctors in Florida advised him not to travel until the end of April or early May:

> And May 28 comes mighty soon to definitely commit on an occasion so important to you and Laura.
>
> I have never felt so honored as to be asked to serve as your best man—damned few grandfathers have been so honored. You made me feel very humble by the invitation and under normal circumstances would grab the chance to feel youthful again—but we both should approach it sensibly and realistically.
>
> So I'd suggest you consider how you have honored me and made me happy in asking. In view of the circumstances, rethink it all over, get someone more in keeping with the wedding party and realize how happy in asking you have made me.

Although he wasn't able to serve as best man, Peyton did add his special touch to the honeymoon. He and Kat provided the newlyweds with their Ocean Reef condo, fully stocked with provisions.

Peyton turned seventy-six on 9 April 1983. There was a big party for him at the country club and Sarah Eich ordered an enormous chocolate cake for the occasion. It was so large that they had to borrow a station wagon to transport it from the caterer's to the club. Jack drove while Laura Nelle sat in back, making sure the cake made the trip unscathed.

Kat's health was worsening. She was no longer able to jet across the Atlantic or shop on Fifth Avenue, but she still took part in weekly bridge games with her friends. And she and Sarah spent endless hours talking and sorting through the thousands of photographs she and Peyton had taken over more than fifty years of marriage. In June she had heart surgery in Birmingham. She returned home weak and frail. The road to recovery seemed to be a very long one.

Cathy Eich graduated from high school in June and, almost immediately, got engaged. Although she was still recuperating from her surgery, Kat eagerly joined with Sarah and her daughter in the planning for the August wedding. She shared reminiscences of her own engagement and wedding and told them about the handmade lace veil she'd bought in England. Fearful she wouldn't be allowed to bring it through Customs, the young Kat McClure had tied it around her waist under her clothes and walked through undisturbed.

"Cathy," Kat said, eyes shining, "I want you to wear my veil in your wedding."

They found the box in storage and Kat opened it to reveal the delicate old garment. Age had discolored the fragile lace, but the three women soaked it over and over in bleach and then spread it out on the lawn in the bright summer sun until it was as white as Cathy's wedding dress.

Kat's health began to fail in early August and she was hospitalized. Peyton demanded that everything possible be done to help her and he asked Sarah to stay with her. With her daughter's wedding only a couple of weeks away, Sarah might have resented being expected to spend so much time at the hospital, but Kat was not just her employer. The two women had become close friends and she wanted to be with her as much as possible.

Peyton was determined that his wife receive the very best care. When he wasn't there, he wanted to know exactly what was happening. He had Sarah keep a daily record of every person who walked in the room. He wanted every pulse, temperature, and blood pressure reading noted, as well as when and how much medication was administered to her.

Kat remained alert and sharp until the point where she finally lapsed into unconsciousness. Just before that happened, she gave Sarah a sad smile.

"I'm going to miss Cathy's wedding."

Katherine McClure Anderson died on 13 August 1983.

Exactly one week later, Cathy Eich was married. She walked down the aisle, her head high and her face framed by Kat's beautiful, smuggled veil.

18

A New Life and an Old Foe

After Kat's death, Peyton grew even closer to the Eichs. Most nights he had dinner with them in the kitchen, and he and Jack often sat up late talking. Eich loved hearing the stories about his service in the Pacific and his friendships with such famous people as Lyndon Johnson and Carl Vinson. Peyton was always pulling out the curiosities and gadgets he'd picked up over the years for the younger man to admire. He was especially fond of watches and had a drawer full—everything from expensive gold timepieces to Mickey Mouse watches. One of his favorite possessions was something he called an umbrella for two. It opened to reveal two umbrellas on one handle.

Although Christmas of 1983 was a sad occasion for him and his family, Peyton still gave gifts to the hundreds of people on his list, with Jack and Juanita distributing the turkey dinners. On New Year's Day, he followed his tradition and hosted his annual Pea Party at his home. Jack and Sarah helped, but he wouldn't let anyone do the cooking but himself. When the party ended, he loaded the leftovers into quart jars and delivered them the next day to people who hadn't been able to attend.

Peyton Anderson was not a man who tolerated loneliness well. He needed to be around people—he always had. He craved companionship. In 1984, he found love again.

He and Evelyn McArver Matthews had known each other for many years. Their families belonged to the same country club. They attended the same parties and knew the same people. She'd been a widow for thirteen years when she and Peyton began seeing each other. Her son Bill Matthews was glad to see his mother so happy and he wasn't surprised when they announced they were planning to marry. He thought it was a fine idea.

The wedding was a very small one. Only Evelyn's sons, Henry and Bill, and their wives, Laura Nelle, her daughter and son-in-law, and Juanita Jordan attended the ceremony in the chapel of the First Presbyterian Church on Mulberry Street. Although Peyton had adamantly told her, "We're not having any flowers. We're not having any pictures," Juanita took a camera along and snapped the couple's picture as they left the chapel.

After the ceremony Jack Eich drove them to the airport where a Knight-Ridder jet waited. On board, an elaborate buffet had been set up for the newlyweds. They flew to the Cotton Bay Club in the Bahamas for a two-week honeymoon. When they returned to Macon, Evelyn moved into the Oakcliff Road house, but it was not the best home for the two of them. They needed a place that was neither his nor hers, but theirs, and finally they bought a large house on Old Club Road South near Idle Hour Country Club. Evelyn sold her Vista Circle house and Peyton put the Oakcliff Road house up for sale.

Jack and Sarah Eich didn't make the move with the Andersons. Instead they returned to their own home. While Jack continued working for Peyton, Sarah went back to her former position in retail sales. She'd grown so close to Kat that she just wasn't comfortable working for Peyton's second wife.

Bill Matthews and his family lived only a few miles from his mother's new house. He and Fran and their children were frequent visitors there, stopping by once or twice a week. Peyton always welcomed them enthusiastically and he especially delighted in being around the children.

His love of gadgets hadn't changed over the years. He was one of the first people in Macon to have a cell phone—a huge, box-like contraption that fit into a cradle in his car. His shopping habits were equally unchanged. One afternoon he and Evelyn were going to visit Bill and Fran. Peyton used the car phone to call them. "We're going by Kroger to pick up some things," he said. "Can we get you anything?"

Fran gave them a short list of items, including Worcestershire sauce, and Peyton reverted to type. He purchased two of almost everything she'd mentioned, including a pair of large bottles of Worcestershire sauce. When he saw them, Bill estimated they now had a five-year supply of the condiment.

Peyton wanted to do everything he could to make his new wife happy. They spent months furnishing their home, and he bought Evelyn a Mercedes convertible because driving it made her feel young and carefree. He also helped her with her investments. Her portfolio hadn't been touched in years and Peyton pushed her to streamline her assets and become a more hands-on investor.

The cancer Peyton had believed to be in remission recurred—this time in his lung and colon. He faced the diagnosis the way he did everything else in his life—head-on, with a determination to win.

"It has been a life of tests, scans and decisions since April 9," he wrote to Reid. "It all boils down to taking radio therapy treatments for my lung cancer starting Monday 6/1. Not much alternative. Keep your chin up—this too will pass.

Bestest, Peyton"

After the radiation treatments, Peyton's strength slowly began to return. By August, his appetite was back and food actually appealed to him again.

He wrote to his granddaughter Laura, "I have improved greatly. It has been a rough time and recovery is slow. A long way to the 6 months they say is necessary to feel good and be active. Am good for about 4 hours, then just give out—physically and in interest."

Peyton and Evelyn spent the Christmas holidays in the Caribbean, but the new year brought them more trouble. Peyton's cancer returned—this time his vocal chords were the targets of the disease—and he suffered through another round of radiation treatments that summer.

In July, the house on Oakcliff Road finally sold, although at a price below the appraised value. After having it on the market for so long, Peyton was just glad to be rid of the responsibility. In a letter to Reid, he wrote of the new owners. "All theirs, lock, stock and barrel. A load off my mind. A lousy financial deal, but I'm emotionally happy that the place is in appreciative hands."

The latest treatments he'd received didn't knock back the cancer, so there was more chemotherapy and radiation to be endured in 1987. Jack would drive him to and from his appointments, helping him in and out of the wheelchair that was now necessary for his mobility. Peyton wasn't sleeping well and many nights he and Jack sat in the den of his house and talked until early morning.

On Peyton's eightieth birthday, most of his family were able to be in Macon. Only three of his grandchildren couldn't come. After the party, he wrote to Adam Bleibtreu, thanking him for being at the party. "The highlights of my 80th birthday were 1) the party, 2) 80 red roses, 3) You, Kattie, Sarah, Deyerle, Larry, Reid, Dr. Laura, Kate, Brad, Laura all being here. I'm a lucky guy to have such great relatives. I know, too, that Josh, Jason and Peyton would have liked to have been here."

As summer finally loosened its grip on Macon and the days grew cool and pleasant, Peyton was spending most of his time at home. He was, however, still in daily contact with his office.

One afternoon his stockbroker called Juanita with the disturbing news that the market was down 365 points. "And I don't know where it's going from here," he said gloomily. "What do you want me to do?"

Juanita was alone in the office and didn't know whether to order the broker to sell or not. She called Peyton at home, hating to be the bearer of such bad news. But her boss was calm about the drop in the market.

"Well, you ride 'em up, you ride 'em down," he said philosophically, and told her to leave the investments where they were.

Peyton lost $10 million in the '87 crash—almost a fourth of his total wealth—but he never complained about it and never second-guessed his decision.

His health rallied somewhat in November, but by then he knew better than to count on anything. He wrote to Knight-Ridder, advising that he planned to retire from their board the following March.

> It was necessary for me to miss the June and September board meetings. While the cause seems to be temporarily arrested, I have no assurances to that effect. A director should have reasonable knowledge that the board and committee meetings and related activities can be attended. I don't feel I have those assurances.
>
> I have been a director since Knight Newspapers went public in 1969. I have enjoyed every minute of my tenure.
>
> Bestest, Peyton.

On December 18, Knight-Ridder issued a press release announcing Peyton's retirement and Alvah Chapman was quoted, "We have reluctantly accepted the request of Peyton Anderson not to stand for reelection to the board. He has served our company very well. We will all miss his wisdom, his good humor and his valuable insights."

Vera Smith, Doc's widow, had been in the nursing home Juanita found for her for several months when her daughter Dorothy Smith Ebert visited her there at Christmas. After returning home to Pennsylvania, Dorothy wrote Peyton a letter:

Dear Mr. Anderson:

Frank and I want to express to you our deep appreciation for what you are doing for my mother. The fact that you are paying her expenses while she is residing at Hillside View means the difference between Mama being satisfied to stay there and being upset about being there. When we visited her the latter part of December, she repeated over and over to us that 'Peyton is taking care of all my expenses'. She doesn't have to worry about money and, to Mama, this is a major factor. Her mind is hazy about many things, but not about this. Our gratitude also extends to Juanita for steering my sister to Hillside View when the situation was desperate and my sister was in need of help.

I can sleep at night knowing that Mama is being taken care of and that she is in a nice place with nice people taking care of her. It takes such a load off my sister's shoulders; and, for that also, I am extremely grateful.

Daddy spent the happiest days of his life with you, Mr. Anderson, and I know now from his Heavenly Home that he is blessing you for your kindness and your generosity to his beloved Vera.

Again, thank you for this wonderful gift you are giving my Mama. God bless you.

Peyton knew in early 1988 that he was losing his battle with cancer, but he wasn't ready to surrender. He wanted to visit Ocean Reef one last time. He and Jack made plans to do so, ordering a van with a wheelchair lift from Dunlap Chevrolet, but by the time the van arrived in Macon, Peyton had suffered another setback and they never made the trip.

After a brief, stabilizing stay in the hospital, he returned home. His wife and daughters wanted to hire a nurse to care for him there, but Peyton wouldn't have it. "Jack'll take care of me," he declared. And Jack did. He moved into a bedroom adjoining Peyton's. For the last forty days of his life, Jack was with him nearly around the clock.

He had a number of visitors those last days. His daughter Deyerle was one of the most faithful. They had time for long, deep talks and she was able to tell him how proud she was of him and the whole family lineage.

Peyton Anderson suffered a fatal heart attack on Sunday morning, 24 April 1988. He was buried after a graveside service at Riverside Cemetery on April 26. The headline on the story in the *Telegraph and News* that day was "Anderson Always Put Friends First." It was a fitting epitaph.

Peyton Anderson accomplished much in his life. He built a strong, independent newspaper, he helped a number of people, and he left truly remarkable descendants. His daughters are strong, independent women full of laughter and the love of life. His grandchildren have grown to be intelligent, talented people in their own right. Katty's four children followed artistic routes. Joshua Bleibtreu is a director of cinematography and has made films all over the world. Adam is the CEO of his own public relations firm. Jason is a photojournalist for a worldwide news service. Sarah, the youngest, is in New York, a successful designer of a line of bags for personal electronic gear.

Deyerle's children are a bit more conservative, but just as accomplished. Reid Hanson is a doctor of veterinary medicine who teaches at Auburn University. Peyton is a surveyor in West Virginia and Laura is an attorney in Atlanta.

Peyton's personal legacy is a rich one.

19

The Legacy

In his will, Peyton Anderson made generous gifts to family members and selected employees, but the bulk of his estate—some $26.6 million—was set apart for the establishment of the Peyton Anderson Foundation. The original trustees were Ed Sell, Jr., John Comer, Ed Sell III, Evelyn Matthews Anderson, and Juanita Jordan. Juanita Jordan was subsequently appointed executive director. When Evelyn Anderson died in September 2002, she left behind a grieving family and a vacancy on the Foundation board. The remaining trustees named Reid Hanson as the new trustee.

The only requirements for the disbursement of the money were that the recipients be 501.3(c) organizations, rather than individuals, and that it be used for the benefit of Macon and Middle Georgia.

Months before he died, Peyton discussed setting up the foundation with Juanita and explained to her the part he expected her to play.

"What kind of projects would you like funded?" she asked.

His eyes almost twinkled when he said, "You'll know. You know me better than anybody else. You'll know what kind of projects. Just make sure the money goes to good doers, not do-gooders."

Juanita had thought she was prepared for what lay ahead, but then Peyton was gone and the Foundation was a reality. She felt, as she put it later, "like somebody had put me in a helicopter and flown me over the ocean and shoved me out." The enormity of the task before them was difficult to comprehend.

She and the other trustees attended meetings of the Southeastern Council of Foundations, hoping to learn how to manage their fledgling organization. Unfortunately, all they learned was that there were as many methods as there were foundations. They realized they were going to have to make up their procedures as they went along.

The Peyton Anderson Foundation started slowly. The beginning guidelines they developed were based on what they knew Peyton Anderson had wanted. He had, for example, always preferred to contribute seed money rather than funds for ongoing operational costs. In keeping with that sentiment, the trustees tried to choose causes that would make a lasting difference.

The Foundation began with an endowment of $26.6 million and it began growing immediately. In the fifteen years it has been in existence, it has given away almost $40 million. Today the fund contains over $85 million, a tribute to the careful management exercised by the board of trustees.

The grants made by the Peyton Anderson Foundation have been diverse and have had a lasting impact on Middle Georgia and the city of Macon. In many cases, such as NewTown Macon, The Community Foundation, and the Peyton Anderson Community Services Building, the Foundation was the driving force behind the projects. The following are some of the most significant grants to date:

$3,750,934—United Way of Central Georgia—Peyton Anderson Community Services Building, Community Resource Center, and fund distribution

$3,355,000—NewTown Macon—revitalization of downtown area

$2,714,000—Tubman African American Museum—creation, construction, and furnishing of new museum

$2,642,000—Macon State College—endowment for two faculty chairs, scholarships, capital campaign

$2,300,000—Mercer University—Convocation Center capital campaign and Medical School library expansion

$2,095,000—Medcen Foundation—Peyton Anderson Health Education Center, Chapel capital campaign, and Children's Hospital equipment

$1,712,500—Georgia Children's Museum—purchase and renovation of building

$1,600,000—Wesleyan College—science building and scholarship fund for teachers

$1,375,000—Museum of Arts and Sciences—Brown's Mount and Museum renovations

$1,332,351—Salvation Army—capital campaign, laundry building, food storage building, mobile disaster unit, and land purchase

$1,250,000—Girl Scouts of Middle Georgia—Camp Martha Johnson

$500,000—Goodwill Industries of Middle Georgia—land and building acquisition for Goodwill Center

$500,000—Communities in Schools of Macon/Bibb County—start up funding for Education First

$491,572—Central Georgia Technical College Foundation—renovations to the Adult Learning Center Headquarters, literacy pilot program, and development office

$375,000—Community Foundation of Central Georgia—start up expenses and regional expansion

$350,000—Theatre Macon—purchase and renovation of building

$250,000—Ocmulgee Heritage Trail—construction drawings

$200,000—100 Black Men of Macon/Middle Georgia—assistance in funding Project Reach scholarship program and youth center renovations

$200,000—Macon Volunteer Clinic—establishment of volunteer medical clinic to serve the working poor

$160,000—American Cancer Society—build Cancer Center and provide services

$156,000—Macon Little Theatre—structural improvements

$115,425—Meals on Wheels of Macon and Bibb County—kitchen enlargement and emergency meals

$100,000—Fort Hawkins Commission—purchase site of original Fort Hawkins to promote community development and tourism

$50,000—Rebuilding Together Macon—warehouse/office

$23,260—Aunt Maggie's Kitchen Table—start up expenses.

Throughout his life, Peyton Anderson was quick to tell people, "You made your money in Macon, you should spend your money in Macon." Peyton Anderson's money is being spent in Macon every day to improve the lives of all the citizens of Middle Georgia.

Bestest

Index